Oracle of Success

How to get there without getting lost

Art Koroma

Published by New Generation Publishing in 2013

Copyright © Art Koroma 2013

First Edition

The author asserts the moral right under the Copyright, Designs and Patents Act 1988 to be identified as the author of this work.

All Rights reserved. No part of this publication may be reproduced, stored in a retrieval system or transmitted, in any form or by any means without the prior consent of the author, nor be otherwise circulated in any form of binding or cover other than that which it is published and without a similar condition being imposed on the subsequent purchaser.

www.newgeneration-publishing.com

 New Generation **Publishing**

Preface

In every chapter of this book, mention has been made of the secret to success which has made fortunes for more than a thousand wealthy people, whom I have carefully analysed over a long period of years. The idea of writing this book started when I was a small boy in a tiny village called Lokomasama, in the northern Provence of Sierra Leone, while I was working with my father in the woods; a place we usually farmed cassava and grand-nut. He brought to my attention the secret to success, more than three decades ago. The canny, lovable old-man carelessly tossed it into my mind. He sat back in his old small wooden bench outside the farm-house, with a merry twinkle in his eyes, and watched carefully to see if I had brains enough to understand the full significance of what he had said to me.

When he saw that I had grasped the idea, he asked if I would be willing to spend years or more, preparing myself to take it to the world of those in search of success who, without the secret, might go through life as failures. I said I would, and with Tejan Koroma's cooperation, I have kept my promise. This book contains the secret to success, after having been put to a practical test by thousands of people, in almost every walk of life. The old-man's idea was that the magic formula, which gave him a stupendous fortune, ought to be placed within reach of people who do not have time to investigate how people make success, and it was his hope that I might test and demonstrate the soundness of the formula through the experience of people in every calling. He believed the formula should be implemented in all public and private places, and expressed the opinion that if it is properly implemented it would revolutionize the entire universe.

'Discovering Oracle of Success—How to get there without getting lost' is a self-help motivational book filled with many inspiring quotes, great lessons, and personal experiences. The book is interactive in the sense that it gets you thinking about your life. As you read, you find yourself analysing exactly where you are in your life, versus where you would like to be. If you are looking for a book with great tips and tools on how to achieve ultimate success, then 'Finding Oracle of Success—How to get there without getting lost' is the book for you.

Table of Content

The Oracle of Success

Preface 3

Introduction 6

Author's Note 9

Renovating an Old House 11

    January (Planning Your Goals) 14

    February (Succeed Your Goals) 25

    March (Creating Success) 36

    April (Motivational Success)... 54

    May (How to Be Successful In Life)............................... 63

    June (The Secret of Success)... 76

    July (Life is a Journey and not a Destination) 89

    August (When One Door Closes another Door Opens). 102

    September (Wisdom to Success) 113

    October (Greatness and Power)...................................... 123

    November (From Poverty to Prosperity) 134

    December (This is the Key to Success) 144

Recapping 156

The Gradual Nature of Success 156

Alphabet of success 158

Never Too Old To Succeed 165

INTRODUCTION

What an exciting, refreshing and desperately needed trend that our culture tends to 'pretty up', the logic of success. But what really separates winners from losers, legends from laggards, is not a stroke of luck or unbounded ambition; it is the capacity to bounce back from life's inevitable setbacks. Oracle of Success is the shrine of ancient quotes and what I believe is another fundamental piece of information that will help you reach success in life. If you are searching for success in this book it is because you are looking for something, something that might be missing in your life, or for that missing piece of the puzzle, and that will motivate you to read and finally understand the HOW and WHY of success.

My definition of Success is quite simple: Achieve everything you wish in life in full harmony with your love/relationships, work, health and spirit. 'Oracle of success' is dedicated to teaching how to succeed in life; how to find your way to where you want to go and then how to achieve the life you want by using something called money (in other words, how to make money). Obviously you need to know where you want to go, but if you still do not know then please do not worry, you will find out as soon as you understand the inner workings of life.

The reason I choose to use the quotes in order to reach you is that I believe it is always good to keep up with the language of Quotations and take advantage of their actual uses and meaning. Oracle of Success will cover many topics of interest, from the very basic to the very advanced, and for that very reason the book is dedicated to you.

I have very ambitious ideas and a strong desire to make this book your reference to achieving your goals! The topics will go from one extreme to another and there are vast areas for personal development, and since life is a big mix of everything, we will go on revealing infallible predictions through the "Oracle of Success", in order to achieve our goals. Most of us are looking for ways to become motivated and inspired. Life is hard and life is also wonderful.

I tell myself, I write because I want to say something true and original about the nature of failure. That is very ambitious — to say something about the human condition that hasn't been written before. On the hard side of life live the people who say life has thrown them a curve ball day in and day out. They see other people who seem to have a life paved in gold, in which they get break after break with everything seemingly going their way.

Everyday people are living a life of pain, stress and heartache wanting things to change. We see our friends, relativities and neighbours who have lost everything they own trying to live the successful life. Many have given up.

It does not have to be this way for you and me. The 'Oracle' is here. There are quotes and statements that can spur success in people who are willing to learn and tap into the knowledge, skills, and abilities that they already possess.

There is not a day that goes by that I do not look for inspiration, motivation, and quotations for success that could change my life. I am sure that many of you feel the same way.

There are quotes about success that will challenge you. There are quotes regarding failure and success that follow each other. There are motivational quotes on overcoming failure. There are positive quotes. There are quotes on the keys to success. There are even some funny inspirational quotes.

The quotes are arranged in calendar order so you can easily read and think about each quote of the day. I honestly recommend that you bookmark this prophecy because it will be a very fun ride that will certainly enhance your journey to success.

Author's Note

Realistically, this life is like a pendulum that swings from side to side, no one knows when or how it will fall. Life itself is a catastrophe. To be candid, I quickly realized very early in life that to be successful in life requires perseverance and determination. There are also other secrets to success, found by working hard. As a small boy, I grew up in a polygamous home. It is quite obvious that things are not always easy in such an environment. After my father shared the idea of the secret to success with me, I looked at the world, and saw that it was shadowed by sorrow and scorched by the fierce fires of suffering. And I looked for the cause. I looked around, but could not find it; I looked in books, but could not find it; I looked within, and found there both the cause and the self-made nature of that cause. I looked again, and deeper, and found the remedy.

I found one Law, the Law of Love; one Life, the Life of adjustment to that Law; one Truth, the truth of a conquered mind and a quiet and obedient heart. And I dreamed of writing a book which should help men and women, whether rich or poor, literate or illiterate, worldly or unworldly, to find within themselves the source of all success, all happiness, all accomplishment, and all truth. And the dream remained with me, and at last became substantial; and now I send it forth into the world on its mission of healing and blessedness, knowing that it cannot fail to reach the homes and hearts of those who are waiting and ready to receive it.

'Oracle of Success' is the ideal developmental experience for people who want to reach new heights and stay there. Preferences may vary but what remains common and finds room in everybody's heart is the desire to be successful in life. So if we all want to be happy and successful, why not work on both together? Earning more money when we are young is like tasting one flavour of success. Now let us taste a few other flavours too; a smile that does not fade, the joy in spreading happiness, enjoyment in every little thing along the way to achieving our goal, and contentment in what we have. 'Oracle of Success' helps us relish all these different flavours and renovates our old house into a success. Let's see how.

Renovating an Old House

Family, friends and I embarked on renovating an old SaintArt style home within a Lokomasama Museum. Trying to whip a three-story house of its size and condition into shape is a trying task, and sometimes we find ourselves both mentally and physically exhausted from the sheer amount of labour involved. Then too, innumerable and unexpected complications arise nearly every day, and any form of progress is painfully slow.

Perhaps to some people, this endeavour would seem mad, but this old house has a load of character and many wonderful qualities that are worth saving, and we're determined to make it a home and preserve something of man's history in the process. Along the way, we've found that there are many lessons to be learned in restoring an old house, which are worth sharing.

Renovating an old house:

Teaches you to be thankful for the simple things that most people take for granted every day—such as running water, electricity, a sound leak proof roof over the head.

Teaches you that there's more than one way to achieve a certain result, and that you sometimes have to alter your plans in order to reach your goal.

Reminds you every day to have reverence for the great things that have passed before you.

Shows you just what you're made of and reveals gifts, talents, and strengths you never knew you had.

Teaches you that with hard work and dedication, you can accomplish the seemingly impossible.

Proves that if you keep working at it, your skills are bound to improve.

Trains your eyes to see beauty that may be difficult to spot under current conditions.

Makes you realize that a house is not a home unless you make it one.

Reveals the importance of working together to achieve a goal.

Makes you stop and think about the importance of spending money wisely and making every cent count.

Reminds you that life does not last forever and that you should make the most of yours during your short time here on earth.

Reveals that everything you do today will affect tomorrow, and that every stone you lay will affect other people's lives.

Proves that aging can be beautiful and has a certain wonderful and unmatchable quality of its own.

Teaches you that someone will always find fault with the way you do things, no matter how well you think you did it, and you learn to live with it and grow from it, and believe in yourself despite it.

Brings you closer to family and friends and reminds you how thankful you are for them and their support.

Gives you a greater appreciation for God, and for all of the minor miracles he performs along the way.

JANUARY
(Planning Your Goals)

The beginning of a New Year is usually the time that people plan their goals for the year ahead, only to forget about them within a few days or weeks into the first month. What is the reason that so few people follow through on their goals and what can you do to make sure that it won't happen to you?

This chapter/month will introduce some points that can help you to stick to your goals and achieve what you desire in the year ahead.

The first thing that you need to do is sit down somewhere quiet and really think about what it is you want. Make sure that it is something you really want and not just something you think you should achieve because everyone else is doing it. Don't just follow the crowd, you must feel a strong emotional commitment to the goal or goals you are setting.

Think about the things that you will need to give up in order to achieve your aims. You also need to consider the actions that you will have to take to get there. For example you may need to learn a new skill. This involves setting aside a certain amount of time every day for studying or practicing whatever it is that you are learning. This may mean cutting back on your TV time. Just remember that every benefit comes with a cost.

One of the main reasons that people fail to keep working at their goals is that they make too many at one time. By making too many goals at once you are setting yourself up for failure, as your thoughts will become scattered and you will feel overwhelmed. When it becomes too much to cope with the result will be to abandon everything, so rather start off with just one or two goals at a time and stick to them.

When planning your goals, be specific and keep track of how you progress. Plan a goal with the end result that you wish to achieve and then go back and set a plan of action, step by step of how you wish to achieve it. Make it challenging but also achievable. Write down your goals with a date by which you intend to have achieved them and exactly how you will get there.

Once you have set up your plan of action and set your dates, keep a record of each step along the path, so that you can see how effectively your plan is working.

Each time you complete a step successfully, give yourself a reward. This helps to encourage and motivate you along the way to ultimate success. Write down what each reward will be along the path to your ultimate goal.

Tell people what your goals are and how you are going to achieve them. The reason for this is that the more people who know the more focused and determined you will be to get there.

Remember also to allow yourself a little bit of leeway when both planning and achieving your goals. Some flexibility is necessary as there are bound to be some occasions when you fall a bit behind. Don't beat yourself up about it, just reschedule your time to make up for the time that you lost, as this way you will not start to think negatively.

Initially put in some extra effort as this will help to establish a routine for you and get you into the habit of working regularly and diligently on your plan of action. Begin by aiming to achieve one or two of your short term goals in the first month or two, which will make it much easier to keep going.

If after working regularly and diligently on your goals, you feel that you are not getting anywhere, then you will need to reassess the situation, see where you have gone wrong, learn from your mistakes and set a new schedule to work towards your ultimate goal

1st January

An optimist stays up until midnight to see the new year in. A pessimist stays up to make sure the old year leaves....The object of a new year is not that we should have a new year. It is that we should have a new soul.

2nd January

You set your goals to a point where they're attainable, but far enough away that you have to really go get them. And every year I push my goals a little bit farther away, and every year I work a little bit harder to get them.

3rd January

I believe that we are who we choose to be. Nobody is going to come and save you. You've got to save yourself. Nobody is going to give you anything, you've got to go out and fight for it. Nobody knows what you want except you, and nobody will be as sorry as you if you don't get it .So don't give up on your dreams.

4ᵗʰ January

If you're climbing the ladder of life, you go rung by rung, one step at a time. Don't look too far up, set your goals high but take one step at a time. Sometimes you don't think you're progressing until you step back and see how high you've really gone.

5ᵗʰ January

No, this is not the beginning of a new chapter in my life; this is the beginning of a new book! That first book is already closed, ended, and tossed into the seas; this new book is newly opened, has just begun! Look, it is the first page! And it is a beautiful one!

6ᵗʰ January

The chief beauty about time is that you cannot waste it in advance. The next year, the next month, the next week, the next day, the next hour are lying ready for you, as perfect, as unspoiled, as if you had never wasted or misapplied a single moment in all your life. You can turn over a new leaf every hour if you choose.

7ᵗʰ January

I will admit that I wanted to shout for standing on the top of a scaffold in front of a good new wall always goes to my head. It is a sensation something between that of an angel let out of his cage into a new sky and a drunkard turned loose in a royal cellar. And after all, what nobler elevation could you find in this world than the scaffold of a wall painter? No admiral on the bridge of a new battleship designed by the old navy, could feel more pleased with himself than Gulley, on two planks, forty feet above dirt level, with his palette table beside him, his brush in his hand, and the draught blowing up his trousers; cleared for action.

8th January

Don't try to be spiritual. That is only a word in the dictionary. Make it your goal to become a normally functioning individual. Let these principles shape you according to your real nature of a simple, decent, honest, unafraid human being.

9th January

I think there is something more important than believing: Action! The world is full of dreamers. There aren't enough who will move ahead and begin to take concrete steps to actualize their vision.

10th January

Gratefulness is the key to a happy life that we hold in our hands, because if we are not grateful, then no matter how much we have it will not make us happy— because we will always want to have something else or something more.

11th January

Truth is the beginning of every good thing, both in heaven and on earth; and he who would be blessed and happy should be from the first a partaker of truth, for then he can be trusted.

12th January

A new day is a privilege to us so we can start afresh, and forget about the worries of yesterday, take the advantage of a new day and make the best out of it, never let your past destroy what comes of tomorrow.

13th January

People grow through experience if they meet life honestly and courageously. This is how character is built.

14th January

Wake up every day knowing that today is a new day and only you can determine the outcome of that day. So dream big and never look back.

15th January

Most people spend more time planning their grocery shopping than designing their future. The basic difference between people who live their dreams and those who only dream about how they would live, are the accuracy of their plans, their ability to generate new ideas, and their ability to take action. Thinking is easy, acting is difficult, and to put one's thoughts into action is the most difficult thing in the world. They say anything is possible, you need to dream as if you've never seen obstacles.

16th January

The total alteration in underlying circumstances has not been squarely faced, As a result, we are guided, in part, by ideas that are relevant to another world... We do many things that are unnecessary, some that are unwise, and a few that are insane.

17th January

When planning for a year, plant corn. When planning for a decade, plant trees. When planning for life, train and educate people.

18th January

The ultimate wisdom which deals with beginnings, remains locked in a seed. There it lies, the simplest fact of the universe and at the same time the one which calls faith rather than reason.

19th January

The best thing you have to offer the world is yourself. You don't have to copy anyone else. If you do, you're second best. To achieve success is to be first, and that's being yourself.

20th January

The Old Year has gone. Let the dead past bury its own dead.

The New Year has taken possession of the clock of time.

All hail the duties and possibilities of the coming twelve months!

Don't wait for something big to occur. Start where you are, with what you have, and that will always lead you into something greater.

21st January

When I face the desolate impossibility of writing 500 pages, a sick sense of failure falls on me, and I know I can never do it. Then gradually, I write one page and then another. One day's work is all that I can permit myself to contemplate.

22nd January

Some stories don't have a clear beginning, middle and end. Life is about not knowing, having to change, taking the moment and making the best of it, without knowing what's going to happen next. Delicious ambiguity.

23rd January

The secret of getting ahead is getting started. The secret to getting started is breaking your complex overwhelming tasks into small manageable tasks and then starting on the first one.

24th January

You better live your best and act your best and think your best today, for today is the sure preparation for tomorrow and all the other tomorrows that follow.

25th January

Success means doing the best we can with what we have. Success is the doing, not the getting; in the trying, not the triumph. Success is a personal standard, reaching for the highest that is in us, becoming all that we can be.

26th January

The greatest thing a man can possibly do in this world is to make the most possible out of the stuff that has been given him. This is success, and there is no other.

27th January

Keep on beginning and failing. Each time you fail, start all over again, and you will grow stronger until you have accomplished a purpose—not the one you began with perhaps, but one you'll be glad to remember.

28th January

Don't look further for answers: be the solution. You were born with everything you need to know. Make a promise to stop getting in the way of the blessing that you are. Take a deep breath, remember to have fun, and begin.

29th January

Aim for success, not perfection. Never give up your right to be wrong, because then you will lose the ability to learn new things and move forward with your life.

30th January

I do not have superior intelligence or faultless looks. I do not captivate a room or run a mile under six minutes. I only succeeded because I was still working after everyone else went to sleep.

31st January

A new day is a new opportunity to take advantage of the plans that you and God have for the rest of your life. A new day is a new beginning, a new chance to look forward to overcoming challenges and obstacles in which you know you will see on a daily basis.

A new day is a chance for you to get wiser, to gain knowledge, and to be able to use the knowledge and wisdom that you learned in the days past, so that each new day will be brighter for you.

A new day is a blessing, so treat it as such. Never take a new day for granted, because we are given every new day, we aren't able to determine when the gift of living new day after new day will be taken away from us. No one lives forever, and ultimately one day will be our last day. Be sure to LIVE your life, and to treat each day as a new day.

Planning is making a schedule or arranging things in order that makes our job easier. Any job needs careful planning which is the first step towards achieving the goal. Before execution, planning the job helps to do it in an organized manner without causing any confusion. "A good plan is like a road map, it shows the final destination and usually the best way to get there" said Stanley Judd. Planning shortens the tedious travel and helps to reach the goal faster and more safely. A man who plans and executes is successful but to think that you can play after the execution is stupidity. Also, the plan should be thought of as soon as a job is at hand to be accomplished. 'A good plan today is better than a perfect plan tomorrow 'said George S. Patton. But it is crucial to plan after a lot of thought and once the planning are framed, we should stick to it firmly without deviating from it. It is idiotic to believe that planning is unnecessary and everything will come by chance. These quotes on planning are very useful for students and those who pursue a career. Read them and share them with your friends.

FEBRUARY
(Succeed Your Goals)

Do you believe that you can succeed? Do you believe that you can reach your goals? That is probably the single most important question that you can ask yourself, because if you don't believe in your own abilities, you are always going to struggle to reach your goals.

Your success in life—regardless of your goals—starts with your belief that you can succeed. Here is how to believe that you CAN succeed at reaching your goals. The problem is that doing something new, reaching out towards a new goal or a new dream can be scary.

All sorts of thoughts and emotions come up and distract you from reaching your goal. You begin to experience doubt, worry, and confusion. You wonder if you are really capable of reaching this goal. This starts a downward spiral that keeps you from ever having the belief in yourself that you need.

But you can change that! Start by looking at your goal and asking yourself these questions:

1. Has anyone else ever done this before? Chances are that someone, somewhere in this big world, has achieved something quite similar to what you want to achieve, right? So that means that your goal is doable! You are capable of achieving the same things as most of the people on this planet.

2. Have you ever done something similar? If so, great! You have already proven to yourself that you can learn new things! If not, you have probably already accomplished some amazing things. Did you learn to ride a bicycle? Drive a car? Balance a checkbook? Use a computer? All of those are amazing skills! Now you simply 'learn' the new skills that you need to reach your goal. Reviewing your past successes is often a great way to build up your belief in yourself.

3. Why do you want it? This is a big question, but if you want to know how to believe that you can succeed, you have to be able to answer it.

If you have a strong reason why you want something, your belief that you can succeed is strengthened. The stronger your belief in yourself, the more you will be willing to do in order to realize your goal. Believe in yourself and your 'self' will never let you down! Know that there will be ups and downs in the road toward your dreams, but also know that as long as you keep moving forward you will eventually get there!

There are numerous quotes that are highly inspirational and motivating in attaining success. Read them and share with your friends and others.If you paint in your mind a picture of bright and happy expectations, you put yourself into a condition conducive to your goal.

1stFebruary

Don't count what you lost but instead cherish what you have and plan what you want to gain, for the past never returns but the future may fulfill the loss.

2nd February

The dictionary is the only place that success comes before work. Hard work is the price we must pay for success. I think you can accomplish anything if you're willing to pay the price.

3rd February

The man who will use his skill and constructive imagination to see how much he can give for a dollar, instead of how little he can give for a dollar, is bound to succeed.

4th February

Nothing can stop the man with the right mental attitude from achieving his goal; nothing on earth can help the man with the wrong mental attitude.

5th February

The greater danger for most of us is not that our aim is too high and we miss it, but that it is too low and we reach it.

6th February

I've missed more than 9000 shots in my career. I've lost almost 300 games. 26 times, I've been trusted to take the game winning shot and missed. I've failed over and over and over again in my life. And that is why I succeed.

7th February

Flaming enthusiasm, backed up by horse sense and persistence, is the quality that most frequently makes for success.

8th February

Taxation is the price we pay for failing to build a civilized society. The higher the tax level, the greater the failure. A centrally planned totalitarian state represents a complete defeat for the civilized world, while a totally voluntary society represents its ultimate success.

9th February

Keep your motivation high, it will help you overcome difficulties in life. Don't expect people to come and solve your problems. You have to make plans for yourself.

10th February

Don't let the opinions of the average man sway you. Dream, and he thinks you're crazy. Succeed, and he thinks you're lucky. Acquire wealth, and he thinks you're greedy. Pay no attention. He simply doesn't understand.

11th February

I dread success. To have succeeded is to have finished one's business on earth, like the male spider, who is killed by the female the moment he has succeeded in courtship. I like a state of continual becoming, with a goal in front and not behind.

12th February

The lessons we learnt from our past actions are no doubt important to guide us. Similarly the plans we have for the future are also important to lead us to desired goals. But often we commit the mistake of allowing our past and future to nullify our present time!

13th February

Once the realization is accepted that even between the closest human beings infinite distances continue, a wonderful living side by side can grow, if they succeed in loving the distance between them which makes it possible for each to see the other whole against the sky.

14th February

Take up one idea. Make that one idea your life - think of it, dream of it, live on that idea. Let the brain, muscles, nerves, every part of your body, be full of that idea, and just leave every other idea alone. This is the way to succeed your goals.

15th February

Something in human nature causes us to start slacking off at our moment of greatest accomplishment. As you become successful, you will need a great deal of self-discipline not to lose your sense of balance, humility, and commitment.

16th February

I have learned that success is to be measured not so much by the position that one has reached in life as by the obstacles which he has had to overcome while trying to succeed.

17th February

We must have a theme, a goal, a purpose in our lives. If you don't know where you're aiming, you don't have a goal. My goal is to live my life in such a way that when I die, someone can say, she cared.

18th February

Once you have decided to become better you will have to have a plan. It doesn't have to be a long, intricate plan. It can be simple. Save a dollar a day. Walk a mile a day and read an article a day. That is a simple plan with achievable goals. Someone is going to develop a plan that will take them into the future of their dreams. Let it be You!

19th February

Success or failure depends more upon attitude than upon capacity, successful men act as though they have accomplished or are enjoying something. Soon it becomes a reality. Act, look, feel successful, conduct yourself accordingly, and you will be amazed at the positive results.

20th February

It has always seemed strange to me... the things we admire in men, kindness and generosity, openness, honesty, understanding and feeling, are the concomitants of failure in our system. And those traits we detest, sharpness, greed, acquisitiveness, meanness, egotism and self-interest, are the traits of success. And while men admire the quality of the first they love the produce of the second.

21st February

Our worldly successes cannot be guaranteed, but our ability to achieve spiritual success is entirely up to us, thanks to the grace of God. The best advice I know is to give those worldly things your best but never your all—reserve the ultimate hope for the only one who can grant it.

22ⁿᵈ February

My message, especially to young people is to have courage to think differently, courage to invent, to travel the unexplored path, courage to discover the impossible and to conquer the problems and succeed. These are great qualities that they must work towards. This is my message to the young people.

23ʳᵈ February

The Internet didn't get invented on its own. Government research created the Internet so that all the companies could make money off the Internet. The point isthat when we succeed, we succeed because of our individual initiative, but also because we do things together.

24ᵗʰ February

We believe a renewed commitment to limited government will unshackle our economy and create millions of new jobs and opportunities for all people, of every background, to succeed and prosper. Under this approach, the spirit of initiative—not political clout—determines who succeeds.

25ᵗʰ February

While the long-term goals of an organization will typically be quite stable, its day-to-day priorities are likely to change, sometimes so gradually that they are not noticed.

26th February

Being yourself is one of the hardest things because it's scary. You always wonder whether you'll be accepted for who you really are. I decided to call my record 'Inside Out' because that's my motto about life. I don't think you ever succeed at trying to be anyone else but who you truly are.

27th February

The wish to acquire more is admittedly a very natural and common thing; and when men succeed in this they are always praised rather than condemned. But when they lack the ability to do so and yet want to acquire more at all costs, they deserve condemnation for their mistakes.

28th February

Everyone who achieves success in a great venture solves each problem as they came to it. They helped themselves. And they were helped through powers known and unknown to them at the time they set out on their voyage. They keep going regardless of the obstacles they met.

29th February

Hard work means the serious and dedicated effort that you have put in, to achieve any short-term or long-term goal in your life. Nothing can be achieved without hard work. Your success is directly proportional to your hard work. If you keep on working consistently towards your goal, the almighty shall also reward you with success in your endeavour. All great achievers were hard-working people with a high level of self-esteem and rigorous planning of short-term and long-term goals. Work hard towards your dream and you shall realize and accomplish it. This might sound like a cliché but is absolutely true that there is no alternative or substitute for hard work. The most desired and awaited things in life never come easy. Susan Powter had once remarked, "Hard work—I mean, does anybody use that term anymore? Laziness doesn't fly. It's all in the practice. It does take work and it isn't easy—but man, the rewards."

~~~~~~~~~~~~~~~~~~~~~~~~~~~~

The reason people don't accomplish their goals is because the goals are not tied closely enough to their sense of self—they don't make someone think, "I was put on this planet to accomplish this goal." If you don't feel that connected to what you're doing, you're simply not going to thrive. Period. End of story.

This applies to every single area of your life: relationships, work, hobbies, skills you want to acquire, health, etc. If you're not super connected in the right ways to your goals, you may get by. You may even "do well." But you're not going to thrive. Thriving happens when you're super aligned with your personal purpose. You could make a mediocre relationship work. You could lose some weight. You could check off a bunch of to-dos at a job you don't really enjoy.

But, what's the point in that?

I can attribute every single goal I've accomplished or area I've thrived in to one simple reality: those things were all absolutely at the core of who I was and who I wanted to be.

MARCH
(Creating Success)

Research consistently demonstrates the power of mindset on behavior change. You can set the most exciting goals, make sure they are smart and engage the most sort after coach, but unless your self-image is in alignment with the behaviors and beliefs required to achieve those goals, you will consistently fall short.

Success is not simply a will power thing. We have to deeply believe in our ability to create successful outcomes and then have the habits to get the work done through self-discipline, diligent practice and preparation.

It all begins with your self-image with specific reference to the goal you have set. For instance, if you have a desire to be a comfortable and natural public speaker but your emotions and thoughts along with the underlying beliefs are all centered on fear and memories of mistakes, you will probably not be natural the next time you speak in public. Because much of our thoughts, emotions and actions are automatic, you would have to do a lot more than deal with conscious outcomes (like behavior) if lasting change is desired. Often, the foundation of our self-image is not conscious; the beliefs, memories, expectations and fears are usually automatic, until we coax them above the surface.

Maxwell Maltz, who wrote the book Psycho Cybernetics (1960) stumbled into this research when he tried to help his patients. As a plastic surgeon he conducted surgeries to help people look better so they could feel better about themselves. He noticed that in some cases people would get the surgery requested and almost immediately have a change in disposition. They would become visibly happier and content with their life. Then there were others who would get a similar requested surgery, to change some aspect of their face or body, who for some reason would have no change in disposition. Some of them even got more despondent after the surgery. He found that very curious.

He also had patients who would come in asking for surgeries that were clearly not needed, to his eyes. The patient would be convinced for instance, that their nose was huge when it was pretty normal.

These responses baffled him and so he began research into this brand new (at the time) area of study in psychology—the self-image. How a person saw their self—the 'sort of person' they were, was pivotal. It is in that perception that all else rests. So if the patient thought of herself as ugly no amount of surgery would make a difference. In spite of 'objective' feedback from trusted sources the person would still hang on to their belief.

How the brain and nervous system supports a person's perception of their self was fascinating to Dr. Maltz. In 1945, he began a new career with his research in psycho-cybernetics. He realized that to really help his patients he had to study their psychology and more specifically he had to help them improve their self-image.

His research provides the scientific foundation for my offerings. Success with creating new habits that help is all about self-image management and mastery.

Dr. Maltz helped his patients with 21-day programs of activity. He found that it took about 21 days for his patients to create a new self-image. And what worked for him has worked for me, my clients and my groups—I am deeply grateful to Dr. Maltz and his findings. Here are some of my favorite quotes below, on creating success:

1st March

No matter how good of a person you are, there will always be someone criticizing you. What do you have to say to your critics, even when the critic is yourself? Do you allow what people say about your work, or your dreams affect you in a negative manner? Will you allow the doubts in your own mind to stop you from getting to the places that you truly have the ability to go.

Don't let your brain stop you by making things seem worse than they really are. When we receive criticism that isn't much more than hate, we have to realize that people will always talk about what we do, as long as we are doing something.

The only way that you won't be criticized is if you live a life without taking much action. We will always have people who come against us, even when we feel like we are doing what we can to help humanity. Just be you! Don't let anyone stop you from being who you really are at heart!

2nd March

It took me a long time not to judge myself through someone else's eyes. When will you take the time out to stop judging yourself? When will you take the time out to realize that you are good enough just the way you are, and that with continual growth you will always be more than good enough, instead of "not quite, but almost good enough" or instead of being someone who was good, but lost themselves along the way.

Get over judgment. Get over the judgments of your peers, and quit acting accordingly. There is so much life out there to explore that we leave from our lives when we choose not to look past the judgment of others, and our own judgments of ourselves.

Be a critic, but only criticize yourself in areas that you know you need to grow. Read books, continue to seek knowledge, and keep experiencing life in as many ways as possible. Continue to grow into yourself, and continue to grow so much that you help others to grow along the way.

3rd March

Don't Judge me by my past. I'm not the past anymore. Accept me for who I am because this is me today. We may all have a past, good thing we also all have today! It is time for people to accept you for who you really are.

Are you struggling in coming to terms with the past, and are you wishing that you had done things differently while you had the chance? Well we all have regrets. We all at certain points at least think about how things might have been if we would have done things a little bit differently.

Some hate the fact that they wasted time, not seeing that if it weren't for the time wasted in their life, they wouldn't value time as much as they do now. Some hate the fact that they loved and lost, not realizing that if they had not loved and lost before, they would never really be able to love and be successful in their relationships later.

4th March

I don't know what your destiny will be, but one thing I do know: The only ones among you who will be really happy are those who have sought and found how to serve.

5th March

Two types of choices seem to me to have been crucial in tipping the outcomes [of the various societies' histories] towards success or failure: long-term planning and willingness to reconsider core values. On reflection we can also recognize the crucial role of these same two choices for the outcomes of our individual lives.

6th March

High achievers simply understand how to set goals that accurately reflect their values, their highest aspirations, and their deepest desires. Once you do that, the achievement of your goals is virtually automatic!

7th March

Never judge yourself through someone else's eyes. When we worry about everyone else's opinion of our lives but our own, we are in big trouble. Life is not long enough to be lived in the hopes of pursuing the acceptance of others, because not only will we never gain the acceptance of every single person we desire to make proud of us, but we will never really have a good chance of showing the world how great we are, as we truly are, perfectly imperfect.

If you have dedicated your life to pleasing everyone else, it is never too late to make the changes you need to make to try and get fulfilment in life by actually acting as yourself throughout the active day to day activities that you participate in.

Don't worry about what everyone else sees, worry about what you see as you look into the mirror each day. Always be sure that you are looking at yourself.

8th March

The future is not a result of choices among alternative paths offered by the present, but a place that is created—created first in the mind and will, created next in activity. The future is not some place we are going to, but one we are creating.

9th March

Set goals and communicate them to the people in charge. Set three to five goals per year and communicate those either in writing or directly to as many people as you can above you. This is a great way of showing management that you are interested in growing.

10th March

When you establish a destination by defining what you want, then take physical action by making choices that move you towards that destination, the possibility for success is limitless and arrival at the destination is inevitable.

11th March

The secret to productive goal setting is in establishing clearly defined goals, writing them down and then focusing on them several times a day with words, pictures and emotions as if we've already achieved them.

12th March

If you don't have a well-thought out dream, you can start by figuring out where you want to go. If you cannot see yourself fairly or accurately represented in the community you live (from restaurants to department stores to clothing choices to conversations at the dinner table) and nothing there makes you feel awake or alive, I suggest you start doing some research on some other communities.

13th March

People are always blaming circumstances for what they are. I don't believe in circumstances. The people who get on in this world are the people who get up and look for the circumstances they want and if they can't find them, make them.

14th March

Setting goals is the first step in turning the invisible into the visible. For many it is hard enough to finally come up with some goals to master. When you finally do come to a knowledge of the goals that you know in your heart you should accomplish, you then have to think about what you are going to do to get there. If you want to stay on task and reach success, you have to continue to stay motivated.

One of the best ways to stay motivated is to apply daily, short term, and long-term goals in your life. Setting these goals is important because they help motivate you by seeing exactly where you want to be in your future, and showing you that slowly but surely, you are getting there. Many things don't come easy in life, and we have to be willing to maintain a diligent, hard working, and most importantly, a consistent resolve in how we attack life on a daily basis. Set goals for yourself, and then do all that you can to get to where you want to be.

15th March

A goal without a plan is just a wish. Out of all of the people in society, only a small percentage of people are willing to make goals, and stick to plans in order to accomplish these goals. Are you tired of feeling as if you are floating along in the world without direction? Does it seem like you work very hard, but still aren't getting to where you hoped you would be by now? Chances are, you aren't taking time to set up goals in your life, and plan to get to them.

When we set goals we empower ourselves by keeping ourselves motivated to turn our dreams into a reality. Setting goals and planning our steps to reach them is the only way to not only see where we want to go in life, but also how to take each step to get there.

Try to set goals and plan to reach these goals by making small obtainable goals that you can conquer daily. Doing so will lead you to your dreams, step by step.

16th March

I'm never going to complain about receiving free early copies of books, because clearly there's nothing to complain about, but it does introduce a rogue element into one's otherwise carefully plotted reading schedule. Being a reader is sort of like being president, except reading involves fewer state dinners, usually. You have this agenda you want to get through, but you get distracted by life events, e.g., books arriving in the mail/World War III, and you are temporarily deflected from your chosen path.

17th March

Creating a new theory is not like destroying an old barn and erecting a skyscraper in its place. It is rather like climbing a mountain, gaining new and wider views, discovering unexpected connections between our starting points and its rich environment. But the point from which we started out still exists and can be seen, although it appears smaller and forms a tiny part of our broad view gained by the mastery of the obstacles on our adventurous way up.

18th March

Never give up without a fight, Never think you aren't good enough. Never let others get to you, but try your hardest in everything you do even though you may feel as though you'll never succeed or constantly fail. The great things in life never come easy.

19th March

Our life is how we make it; right decisions, wrong decisions, and we made our choices according to circumstances, ambitions, and purposes. At the end of the day, we have to accept the result of our decisions. Good or bad, we have to deal with it responsibly. Life is a matter of choice, faith, and right attitude to deal our everyday lives.

20th March

The quality of your life is dependent upon the quality of the life of your cells. If the bloodstream is filled with waste products, the resulting environment does not promote a strong, vibrant, healthy cell life-nor a biochemistry capable of creating a balanced emotional life for an individual.

21st March

Don't wait until everything is just right. It will never be perfect. There will always be challenges, obstacles and less than perfect conditions. So what. Get started now. With each step you take, you will grow stronger and stronger, more and more skilled, more and more self-confident and more and more successful.

22nd March

No matter what your situation is, you can become a successful person today. You may not be able to reap the rewards yet, but you can start planting the seeds.

23rd March

You can neither lie to a neighbourhood park, nor reason with it. 'Artist's conceptions' and persuasive renderings can put pictures of life into proposed neighbourhood parks or park malls, and verbal rationalizations can conjure up users who ought to appreciate them, but in real life only diverse surroundings have the practical power of inducing a natural, continuing flow of life and use.

24th March

[Public housing projects] are not lacking in natural leaders,' [Ellen Lurie, a social worker in East Harlem] says. They contain people with real ability, wonderful people many of them, but the typical sequence is that in the course of organization leaders have found each other, gotten all involved in each others' social lives, and have ended up talking to nobody but each other. They have not found their followers. Everything tends to degenerate into ineffective cliques, as a natural course. There is no normal public life. Just the mechanics of people learning what is going on is so difficult. It all makes the simplest social gain extra hard for these people.

25th March

Actual philosophers... are commanders and law-givers: they say "thus it shall be!", it is they who determine the Wherefore and Whither of mankind, and they possess for this task the preliminary work of all the philosophical labourers, of all those who have subdued the past they reach for the future with creative hand, and everything that is or has been becomes for them a means, an instrument, a hammer. Their "knowing" is creating, their creating is a law giving, their will to truth is will to power. Are their philosophers today? Have there been such philosophers? Must there not be such philosophers?

26th March

A gesture cannot be regarded as the expression of an individual, as his creation (because no individual is capable of creating a fully original gesture, belonging to nobody else), nor can it even be regarded as that person's instrument; on the contrary, it is gestures that use us as their instruments, as their bearers and incarnations.

27th March

Great athletes train their minds as well as their bodies. There are various mental conditioning techniques many use when preparing for an event. Perhaps the best known technique is visualization, creating a mental image not only of the desired result (the gold medal, a new world record, a hole-in-one), but also of every move that will be taken en route to the ultimate goal.

28th March

In those instances where two or three individuals of similar skills interview for the same job, it's been shown that the individual who is often extended the offer is the one who communicates the best. In fact, there are times that an individual with a lesser skill set will get the job simply because of his or her communication abilities.

If you communicate well, you have the competition beat by a mile. The question then is whether or not you're fostering good communication in everything you do.

29th March

A city street equipped to handle strangers, and to make a safety asset, in itself, of the presence of strangers, as the streets of successful city neighbourhoods always do, must have three main qualities: First, there must be a clear demarcation between what is public space and what is private space. Public and private spaces cannot ooze into each other as they do typically in suburban settings or in projects.

Secondly, there must be eyes upon the street, eyes belonging to those we might call the natural proprietors of the street. The buildings on a street equipped to handle strangers and to insure the safety of both residents and strangers, must be oriented to the street. They cannot turn their backs or blank sides on it and leave it blind.

And third, the sidewalk must have users on it fairly continuously, both to add to the number of effective eyes on the street and to induce the people in buildings along the street to watch the sidewalks in sufficient numbers. Nobody enjoys sitting on a stoop or looking out a window at an empty street. Almost nobody does such a thing. Large numbers of people entertain themselves, off and on, by watching street activity.

30th March

Only hard work pays. If at all luck plays a role it is only temporary. Aristotle says, "It is possible to fail in many ways while for success it is possible only in one way". Hurdles and failures are the stepping stones to success and from failure to failure we have to proceed with unquenched enthusiasm and zeal to attain success in our endeavours.

Arnold Glasgow gives the simplest route to success thus "success is simple. Do what's right the right way at the right time". The above numerous 'quotes' are highly inspirational and motivating in attaining success.

31ˢᵗ March

Don't let yourself be controlled by these three things: your past, people and money. Sometimes we live our lives In such a hurried pace in order to "Secure" ourselves with money and stability that things we once had to consider aren't even considered choices any longer. The people that we use to love have been pushed aside for those who only truly desire to control us so that we may live lives pleasing to them.

Instead of letting things you can't control about your past hold you back from pursuing your dreams, and instead of letting people and money dominate your thoughts and actions, listen to your heart, and to who you really are, the person that God made you to be.

Never doubt yourself! We waste so much time doubting that we eventually start to feel confused not knowing what things are really right, and what things aren't! Take control of your life today, and each day. Become empowered and work hard to get where you need to be for the right reasons!

To live a creative life, we must lose our fear of being wrong. Being creative is all about being as radical as possible. Not in the sense of we should fight the government or anything, but in the sense of we should be ourselves in everything that we do, with no holds barred. We simply don't have time to waste trying to be right; all that we should focus our time on being is ourselves to the max.

Living creatively requires a person to understand that they don't have to do things to fit in, and that they shouldn't try to do things just for the sake of standing out either. Just do the things that you feel are right in your heart, and right in your gut to do. Take risks, and take chances. Seize every day as if it is yours, because it is yours. Remember that over time the people that were remembered were those who stood up for what they believed in and presented a real picture of themselves to the world, not those who simply just tried to fit in and let others think and do things for them!

~~~~~~~~~~~~~~~~~~~~~~~~~~~~~~

It's so funny how the people who know the least about you, have the most to say. One of the funniest things in life is receiving judgment from a person who has no clue about your life. When you start to see people taking a big interest in your life, and when you start to see people judging you from where you are going, and from what they see at a distance, then you really know that you are on to something big.

People don't hate too often on things that they don't see having a future, or things that they don't see becoming a success. They give hate because they know that if you continue to do what you are doing, you will be a success, and often times they aren't or won't continue to be a success because they aren't able to adapt like you are.

So when you hear them talking about you, use it as encouragement. You are blessed, and on your way to great things, and a successful life!

APRIL
(Motivational Success)

Motivation around the clock! This chapter is an Inspirational Community for Self Growth, through tools, collaboration and life changing connections. Inspiring people around the world to achieve their greatness.

To achieve more, be a person of action. Throughout your day keep in mind the old saying, "all else fails without action". As you put forth effort on the things you deem to be most worthwhile, you will find that your inner belief system grows.

The beliefs you hold about yourself determine the goals you are able to manifest in your life. Dream big, for when you do, truly you will see that your life becomes one filled with rich life experiences.

The following quotes are not necessarily quotes from great leaders or inspiring statements that might be used by leaders. Rather, they are but wisdom that might be applied to the process of becoming a great leader (or parent). They represent food for thought, fodder to consider daily.

An attempt has been made to "categorize" the quotes into three general areas, Leadership, Success and Personal, for the purpose of search efficiency. Interestingly, so many of the elements that lend themselves to either personal or professional success share a common thread, therefore, categorizing has been difficult at best and many of the quotes may seemed wrongly categorized.

Credit has been extended whenever possible to the authors, the value of each quote as a component of public domain and as a treasure is recognized in all cases. We hope you enjoy and perhaps can benefit from the short selection of quotes to follow.Read and share these quotes on motivation which will be highly useful.

1stApril

We don't need more strength or more ability or greater opportunity. What we need is to use what we have.
We are what we repeatedly do. Excellence, therefore, is not an act but a habit.

2ndApril

The great successful men of the world have used their imagination. They think ahead and create their mental picture in all its details, filling in here, adding a little there, altering this a bit and that a bit, but steadily building—steadily building.

3rdApril

Would you like me to give you a formula for success? It's quite simple, really. Double your rate of failure. You are thinking of failure as the enemy of success. But it isn't at all. You can be discouraged by failure or you can learn from it, So go ahead and make mistakes. Make all you can. Because remember that's where you will find success.

4th April

Go to the people. Learn from them. Live with them. Start with what they know. Build with what they have. With the best of leaders, when the job is done, when the task is accomplished, the people will say we have done it ourselves.

5th April

Rely on your own strength of body and soul. Take for your star self-reliance, faith, honesty and industry. Don't take too much advice—keep at the helm and steer your own ship, and remember that the great art of commanding is to take a fair share of the work. Fire above the mark you intend to hit. Energy, invincible determination with the right motive, is the levers that move the world.

6th April

We distinguish the excellent man from the common man by saying that the former is the one who makes great demands on himself, and the latter who makes no demands on himself.

8th April

Possess the focus and determination to take action on your ideas that often start out as simple thoughts, and realize as they are fulfilled you are building momentum that can often transform your life into much more than you ever imagined.

9th April

It's possible to go on, no matter how impossible it seems, and that in time, the grief ... lessens. It may not go away completely, but after a while it's not so overwhelming.

10th April

Don't say you don't have enough time. You have exactly the same number of hours per day that were given to Martin Luther King Jr., Malcolm-X, Michelangelo, Mother Teresa, Leonardo da Vinci, Thomas Jefferson, and Albert Einstein.

11th April

You must accept that you might fail; then, if you do your best and still don't win, at least you can be satisfied that you've tried. If you don't accept failure as a possibility, you don't set high goals, you don't branch out, you don't try—you don't take the risk.

12th April

A man can be as great as he wants to be. If you believe in yourself and have the courage, the determination, the dedication, the competitive drive and if you are willing to sacrifice the little things in life and pay the price for the things that are worthwhile, it can be done.

13th April

Anything in this world is possible and you have the capacity to acquire all that you set your sights on. Believe in yourself, you possess the inner drive to accomplish all of your desires. If you commit yourself entirely to the things you want and maintain the strength to follow through, you will succeed in reaching your goals.

14th April

Overcome the obstacles you may face in accomplishing something you may not be 100% familiar with. The knowledge and experience needed can easily be learned, especially if you break the action down into smaller parts and then concentrate on each of them one at a time.

15th April

There is no better time than now. The time to live is now. The time to dream is now. The time to imagine and forget the past is now. The time to shine is now. The time to bleed, sweat, and determine yourself for the things you want most is now.

16th April

Always avoid the mistake of setting out for something without approaching it or concentrating on it fully. Take affirmative action. As you set out to accomplish the things you most desire, really hold yourself accountable to completing all the necessary tasks that will lead you toward your ultimate goal.

17th April

People spend a lifetime searching for happiness; looking for peace. They chase idle dreams, addictions, religions, even other people, hoping to fill the emptiness that plagues them. The irony is the only place they ever needed to search was within.

18th April

It isn't about how hard you hit. It's about how hard you can get hit and keep moving forward. How much you can take and keep moving forward. That's how winning is done! Now if you know what you're worth then go out and get what you're worth.

19th April

When you're struggling with something, look at all the people around you and realize that every single person you see is struggling with something, and to them, it's just as hard as what you're going through.

20th April

Be wise to insure that every idle word spoken is carried with peace, driven with love, and filled with hope. For this we know is certain, one day our words will become our last.

21st April

You know you're doing what you love when Sunday nights feel the same as Friday nights....

22nd April

I learned this, at least, by my experiment; that if one advances confidently in the direction of his dreams, and endeavors to live the life which he has imagined; he will meet with a success unexpected in common hours.

23rd April

Always be proactive in getting your most important tasks done first. Procrastination often sets in when we worry about too many things at once, many of them often not important enough to even complete in the first place. Prioritize what really needs to be done, and you will soon find you have more than enough time to do it all.

24th April

A clay pot sitting in the sun will always be a clay pot. It has to go through the white heat of the furnace to become porcelain.

25th April

Until we take how we see ourselves (and how we see others) into account, we will be unable to understand how others see and feel about themselves and their world. Unaware, we will project our intentions on their behavior and call ourselves objective.

26th April

It takes a great deal of strength of character to apologize quickly from one's heart rather than out of pity. A person must possess himself and have a deep sense of security in fundamental principles and values in order to genuinely apologize.

27th April

People can't live with change if there's not a changeless core inside them. The key to the ability to change is a changeless sense of who you are, what you are about and what you value. —The 7 Habits of Highly Effective People.

28th April

Though a good motive cannot sanction a bad action, a bad motive will always vitiate a good action. In common and trivial matters, we may act without motives, but in momentous ones the most careful deliberation is wisdom.

29th April

Take control of your destiny. Believe in yourself. Ignore those who try to discourage you. Avoid negative sources, people, places, things and habits. Don't give up and don't give in. Your life isn't behind you; your memories are behind you. Your life is always right here, right now. Seize it! Choose to let each of your experiences today be a gateway to an even brighter tomorrow.

30th April

Motivation is the inspiration or the stimulus that acts as a driving force behind any action. Reading the above quotes on motivation helps to give a lift when our spirits are down. Motivation can come in the form of words, actions or advice from others.

It is almost impossible to be in the highest of spirits all time, all day. So, everyone needs some kind of motivation either in the work place, at home or even when they are alone. The external factors that influence in bringing down our spirits can be successfully overcome by reading quotes on motivation.

"Do not wait to strike till the iron is hot, but make it hot by striking". Motivation helps even an inefficient person to record great achievements. We have all heard of Robert Bruce who even after failing seventeen times in war was motivated by a small spider.

~~~~~~~~~~~~~~~~~~

I know and you know that you have more energy, strength, power and awesomeness than you can imagine, nothing or nobody can stop you from achieving whatever you desire; but you and your self-belief. So focus on your belief in your ability, your skill and yourself.

MAY
(How to Be Successful In Life)

Success is about getting all that you wanted to have. It's finding that you have achieved your goals or fulfilled your plans and it's waking up in the morning feeling victorious rather than feeling defeated.

The feelings success brings will make you walk proudly in the streets with your head up high whilst being <u>happy</u> and satisfied.

How to Be Successful in Life
Contrary to common beliefs, there are no successful or unsuccessful people but instead there are people who have the potential to succeed and who do things that help them realize this potential, and there are people with the same potential who don't do those things.
The only thing you need to do to succeed is to do exactly what successful people have done. When you go through all of the information below you will acquire the mentality of a successful person and this will help you reach success.

What Makes Me Unsuccessful?
If you really want to be successful then you should have a solid understanding of certain concepts that can limit your potential and that can make you unsuccessful. Successful people avoid these harmful concepts and so should you:

False Beliefs: False beliefs are incorrect ideas you hold about something or about yourself. An example of a false belief could be "I can never find a job in such a country". False beliefs act as limiters to your true potential and so to your success. Getting rid of false beliefs and knowing more about them is the most important task that you should undertake, if you are serious about success. False beliefs can not only limit your success potential but they can even ruin your life. Some people stay broken for years after a breakup just because they have some false beliefs about love that they acquired from the media.

In this chapter 'how to get over anyone in a few days' I explained how getting rid of false beliefs such as "the one" and "the soul mate" can help you recover in a few days. This happens because the mind refuses to recover if you believe that you will never find a replacement for the person you broke up with. (Check out this month/chapter for more information on false beliefs, how they are acquired and how to get rid of them).

External Locus of Control: This is the way of thinking that makes a person assume that everything that happens to him/her is the result of external factors. For example: saying that an exam was too hard when you don't do well or claiming that high unemployment rate is the reason you can't find a job are examples of external locus of control.

The flip side to that way of thinking is Internal Locus of Control which is the way of thinking that makes you believe that you are in charge and in control of everything that happens to you. No successful person has an external locus of control, so if you are serious about success you should learn how to change your way of thinking; from being based on external locus of control to being based on internal locus of control. (The quotes below will help consolidate your knowledge, on how you can do it.)

1ˢᵗ May

When this business was founded, it sought to win public confidence through service, for it was my conviction then, as it is now, that nothing else than right service to the public results in mutual understanding and satisfaction between customer and merchant.

2ⁿᵈ May

One of the lessons that I grew up with was to always stay true to yourself and never let what somebody else says distract you from your goals. And so when I hear about negative and false attacks, I really don't invest any energy in them, because I know who I am.

3ʳᵈ May

Are you excited to get up in the morning? People with a passion are, and they're energized about what they are doing. You need to live and breathe what it is that you want, and be passionately invested in both the journey and the goal.

4ᵗʰ May

Surround yourself with a group of people who want you to succeed. They will move with you toward your goal. Choose and bond with people who have skills, talents and abilities that you do not. Winners give and receive by being part of other people's nuclear groups.

5th May

Have unwavering faith in yourself, for good and bad. Make the decision to believe that you create all your experiences. You will experience successes thanks to you, and you will experience pain, struggle, and strife thanks to you. Sounds a little strange, but accepting this level of responsibility is uniquely empowering. It means you can do, change, and be anything. Stumbling blocks become just that, little hills to hop over.

6th May

Working for excellence and not success is invokes, invigorates, ignites, inspires an indefatigable motivation within us to encourage, energize, enthuse, enrich and empower environment inside and outside.

7th May

People I work with are open to leadership that has a vision, but this vision has to be communicated clearly and persuasively, and always, always with passion.

8th May

Dream big. It's the first step to success. Just like that saying, shoot for the moon, even if you miss you'll land among the stars. So aim high, aim higher than you ever thought you could because if it just wasn't meant to be, you'll still shine.

9th May

You control the ultimate result of where you will end up, what you may become and how successful you may be. No matter what our current circumstances are, always maintain a strong belief in your abilities to succeed and you will accomplish anything that you set out for.

10th May

An average person with average talent, ambition and education, can outstrip the most brilliant genius in our society, if that person has clear, focused goals.

11th May

I try to learn from the past, but I plan for the future by focusing exclusively on the present. That's where the fun is. And if it can't be fun, what's the point?

12th May

My goal is to help you understand what is "really" happening, the long energetic history that is just now being revealed. Then we will have the power to change things from the source, and the world itself will change.

13th May

Develop an attitude of gratitude, and give thanks for everything that happens to you, knowing that every step forward is a step toward achieving something bigger and better than your current situation.

14th May

Energy is the essence of life. Every day you decide how you're going to use it by knowing what you want and what it takes to reach that goal, and by maintaining focus.

15th May

Success is failure turned out, the silver tint of the clouds of doubt, and you can never tell how close you are, it may be near when it seems afar, so stick to the fight when you are hardest hit, it's when things get worse that you mustn't quit!

16th May

The road to success is not straight. There is a curve called Failure, a loop called Confusion, speed bumps called Friends, red lights called Enemies, caution lights called Family. You will have flat tires called Jobs, but if you have a spare called Determination, an engine called Perseverance, a driver called Will Power, you will make it to a place called Success.

17th May

I don't care how much power, brilliance or energy you have, if you don't harness it and focus it on a specific target, and hold it there, you're never going to accomplish as much as your ability warrants.

18ᵗʰ May

I think there's confusion around what the point of social networks are. A lot of different companies characterized as social networks have different goals - some serve the function of business networking, some are media portals. What we're trying to do is just make it really efficient for people to communicate, get information and share information.

19ᵗʰ May

I will persist until I succeed. Always will I take another step. If that is of no avail I will take another, and yet another. In truth, one step at a time is not too difficult.... I know that small attempts, repeated, will complete any undertaking.

20ᵗʰ May

What I can say generally is that our goal is not to build an operating system from scratch, or else not to design hardware from scratch. Our goal is to make it so that we can design the best integrations in the widest variety of phones.

21ˢᵗ May

In life, it is rarely about getting a chance; it is about taking a chance. You'll never be 100% sure it will work, but you can always be 100% sure doing nothing won't work. Most of the time you just have to go for it! And no matter how it turns out, it always ends up just the way it should be. Either you succeed or you learn something. Win-Win.

22nd May

Before you start some work, always ask yourself three questions—Why am I doing it, What the results might be and Will I be successful? Only when you think deeply and find satisfactory answers to these questions, go ahead.

23rd May

Success or failure depends more upon attitude than upon capacity. Successful men act as though they have accomplished or are enjoying something. Soon it becomes a reality. Act, look, feel successful, conduct yourself accordingly, and you will be amazed at the positive results.

24th May

Don't ask yourself what the world needs; ask yourself what makes you come alive. And then go and do that. Because what the world needs are people who have come alive.

25th May

All successful people men and women are big dreamers. They imagine what their future could be, ideal in every respect, and then they work every day toward their distant vision, that goal or purpose.

26th May

I weep for the liberty of my country when I see at this early day of its successful experiment that corruption has been imputed to many members of the House of Representatives, and the rights of the people have been bartered for promises of office.

27th May

I didn't see it then, but it turned out that getting fired from Apple was the best thing that could have ever happened to me. The heaviness of being successful was replaced by the lightness of being a beginner again, less sure about everything. It freed me to enter one of the most creative periods of my life.

28th May

I've always taught that a poor economy is the best opportunity for salespeople because the naysayers and grumblers have already given up, leaving more territory, more opportunities to be successful than in a good economy when virtually all salespeople are out there, giving it their best.

29th May

Commitment is a big part of what I am and what I believe. How committed are you to winning? How committed are you to being a good friend? To being trustworthy? To being successful? How committed are you to being a good father, a good teammate, a good role model? There's that moment every morning when you look in the mirror: Are you committed, or are you not?

30th May

It is always darkest before dawn. The cliffs are the highest just before the vertex. Why would you want to stand at the bottom and dream of glories when all you need to do is take that next step into the skies and be successful in life? It's not easy to take chances and take blind steps into the clouds, but it's the belief in yourself that can bring miracles. And miracles don't really exist anyways, it's the way you subconsciously bring yourself to the point when you bump into a miracle that was just waiting for you in your path.

And when you climb mountains, you are bound to bump into miracles and into your worst fears, but ask the people who made it to the apex, they'll tell you how sweet success can taste. And is it worth the effort to take that next step, especially when the path is so treacherous? Well, you'll never know until you take that next step. And be what you were born to be.

31st May

Some people dream of success, others make it happen. Are you going to be a person who wants nothing out of life and chooses to sit there and let it pass you by? Are you going to be a person who wants everything out of life, and has the dreams to take his or her self there, but never actually reaches out to grab them? Or are you going to be a go-getter, someone who is willing to grab life by the horns on a daily basis and seize each day.

There are a few things that we could all do to become and maintain our lives as those who are willing to go after their dreams. For example, one may be concerned with a vast array of projects, but in order to get the ball rolling one must be able to prioritize and complete the most difficult tasks first. Another tip that you will need on the road to success is that you have to avoid being a perfectionist, and at the same time avoiding procrastination is key as well. The main ingredient to success is a person's courage and their will to go after their dreams.

Variety is the spice of life and a smooth life without any challenges is boring. Great people take hurdles in their path as challenges and win over them and achieve greatness. Challenges are essential in our life to prove our worth as they help to hone our skills. They are stepping stones to climb the ladder of victory.

Challenges help us to grow; challenges bring out the best in us; challenges make our life adventurous and interesting and hence are an essential part of our life. You would become just another living being if you just tread the path travelled by others; try finding a new path and travel on it to find new places and glories, even if there are challenges you have to overcome. This will leave an indelible mark and earn fame of success.

JUNE
(The Secrets of Success)

Many people want to be successful in their lives for more personal fulfillment and joy. The definition of success can have a different meaning for everyone. Although everyone has their own way of finding success, there are certain things that you need to be aware of in order to have more joy and fulfillment. Make a habit of practicing these **fourteen points** so that you can be the rock star of your life!

1. Do something you are afraid of doing everyday – When you make a habit of getting outside of your comfort zone, you will grow strong mentally and emotionally and will see yourself getting past many mental blocks.

2. Don't over-plan - There is nothing wrong with planning your goals in life, however if you try to perfect your planning, you won't take action on any of your goals.

3. Meet new people – When you constantly meet new people, you will see yourself learning a lot about yourself and others as well. You can then use the new knowledge to contribute and help others.

4. Practice being present - When you are engaged in a specific task/activity or are having a conversation with someone, make sure that you are fully present and not caught up thinking about the past or future.

5. Take leadership roles – Start taking leadership roles in every area of your life. Organize a workshop or plan a trip or a social event. When you start taking leadership roles, your self-confidence will rise.

6. Note down all of your ideas - Whenever an idea pops into your head make sure to write it down somewhere so you can refer back to it. There are going to be those times when your mind will suddenly get creative ideas, so make sure that you have a pen and paper handy.

7. Set aside "alone time" - Spend a half hour every day by yourself in a quiet place and take time to think about your goals for the future. Think about where you want to be in the next ten years.

8. Spend more time outdoors - Get outside the house/office more often. You don't have to plan a big trip to get out. It can be as simple as going for a hike or walking by the beach. You will be able to think clearly and focus better on your tasks. Don't become a workaholic and burn out.

9. Attend seminars - Start attending helpful workshops and seminars of topics that interest you. You will be surprised by the knowledge you will gain. You will also meet like-minded people and make new friends.

10. Read more often - Turn off the television and start reading more. Once you start developing a habit of reading, you will notice that your vision will expand and you will see the world in a whole different way.

11. Don't talk about yourself too much – If you are ever interacting with close friends or at a social event, don't make a habit of talking about yourself and your success. This is a sign of insecurity. Instead, take interest in others unless or until someone asks you more about what you do.

12. Spend minimum time browsing the web – When you constantly browse the web, your mind will be cluttered with different images and thoughts and you will get sidetracked from all your goals.

13. Go to the gym at least four times a week - When you make a habit of working out frequently you will have a lot of positive energy that will help you in other areas of your life. Put it on your calendar and make it a "must do" task.

14. Don't delay to have fun - Some people think that they need to have a lot of money in order to have fun. They think that one day that big paycheck will solve all the problems in life. Life will have its ups and downs regardless of whether you have accumulated a lot of wealth. Don't wait for that big day to arrive to have all your fun. Enjoy every minute of life.

1st June

When I woke up this morning, lying in bed, I was asking myself, 'What are some of the secrets of success in life?' I found the answer right there, in my very room. The fan said...Be Cool. The Roof said...Aim High. The window said...See the World. The Clock said...Every minute is precious. The Mirror said...Reflect before you act. The Calendar...Be up-to-date. The door said...Push hard for your goals.

2nd June

You can never give up and never quit because if you really think about it, there are a multitude of other people who are relying on you to excel and succeed in achieving your goals and objectives.

3rd June

The secret of success is learning how to use pain and pleasure instead of having pain and pleasure use you. If you do that, you're in control of your life. If you don't, life controls you.

4th June

People become really quite remarkable when they start thinking that they can do things. When they believe in themselves they have the first secret of success.

5th June

Follow your dream as long as you live, do not lessen the time of following desire, for wasting time is an abomination of the spirit.

6th June

The only thing standing between you and your goal is the bullshit story you keep telling yourself as to why you can't achieve it.

7th June

Thoughts and ideas are the source of all wealth, success, material gain, all great discoveries, inventions and achievement.

8th June

The dreams that you hold for your future are what you dream about at night. They're always at the back of your mind. They're what your heart desires. They keep you going. Accept reality and have a backup plan, but always follow your dreams no matter what.

9th June

It's not that some people have willpower and some don't. It's that some people are ready to change and others are not.

10th June

The proclivity and the penchant of a man's persistence for doing work par excellence is a great way to improve his prospect, prudence, positivity, productivity, performance and personality both on the personal and professional field.

11th June

It's so important to believe in yourself. Believe that you can do it, under any circumstances. Because if you believe you can, then you really will. That belief just keeps you searching for the answers, and then pretty soon you get it.

12th June

Obstacles don't have to stop you. If you run into a wall, don't turn around and give up. Figure out how to climb it, go through it, or work around it.

13th June

I think people that have a brother or sister don't realize how lucky they are. Sure, they fight a lot, but they know that there's always somebody there, somebody that's family.

14th June

The leaders we revere and the businesses that last are generally not the result of a narrow pursuit of popularity or personal advancement, but of devotion to some bigger purpose. That's the hallmark of real success. The other trapping of success might be the by-product of this larger mission, but it can't be the central thing.

15th June

Your goal of success is, to be very honest with yourself about who you are and what you want out of your life. Spend time thinking about what your purpose is in life. When you are aligned with your purpose in life, you won't get many conflicting thoughts that will leave you confused about who you are.

16th June

I've come to embrace the notion that I haven't done enough in my life. I've come to confirm that one's title, even a title like president of your country, says very little about how well one's life has been led. No matter how much you've done or how successful you've been, there's always more to do, always more to learn, and always more to achieve.

17th June

That's what building a body of work is all about. It's about the daily labour, the many individual acts, the choices large and small that add up over time, over a lifetime to a lasting legacy. It's about not being satisfied with the latest achievement, the latest gold star, because the one thing I know about a body of work is that it's never finished. It's cumulative. It deepens and expands with each day you give your best. You may have setbacks and you may have failures, but you're not done. You haven't even started.

18th June

Don't let the fear of the time it will take to accomplish something stand in the way of your doing it. The time will pass anyway; we might just as well put that passing time to the best possible use.

19th June

The great French Marshall Lyautey once asked his gardener to plant a tree. The gardener objected that the tree was slow growing and would not reach maturity for 100 years. The Marshall replied, "In that case, there is no time to lose. Plant it this afternoon!"

20th June

Dream lofty dreams, and as you dream, so shall you become. Your vision is the promise of what you shall one day be; your ideal is the prophecy of what you shall at last unveil.

21st June

When I was younger I thought success was something different. I thought, "When I grow up, I want to be famous. I want to be a star. I want to be in movies. When I grow up I want to see the world, drive nice cars. I want to have groupies." But my idea of success is different today. For me, the most important thing in your life is to live your life with integrity and not to give into peer pressure, to try to be something that you're not. To live your life as an honest and compassionate person. To contribute in some way.

22ⁿᵈ June

Most people give up just when they're about to achieve success. They quit on the one yard line. They give up at the last minute of the game, one foot from a winning touchdown.

23ʳᵈ June

Success is not measured by what a man accomplishes, but by the opposition he has encountered and the courage with which he has maintained the struggle against overwhelming odds.

24ᵗʰ June

The winners in life think constantly in terms of I can, I will, and I am. Losers, on the other hand, concentrate their waking thoughts on what they should have or would have done, or what they can't do.

25ᵗʰ June

If people ask me for the ingredients of success, I say one is talent, two is stubbornness or determination, and third is sheer luck. You have to have two out of the three. Any two will probably do.

26ᵗʰ June

You have to set goals that are almost out of reach. If you set a goal that is attainable without much work or thought, you are stuck with something below your true talent and potential.

27th June

While starting your journey on the way to success, don't pray for an easy path, rather be determined to keep walking even with hurt teeth and a wounded body, less hope and more disappointments. Just don't stop and it will be yours.

28th June

There are plenty of teams in every sport that have great players and never win titles. Most of the time, those players aren't willing to sacrifice for the greater good of the team. The funny thing is, in the end, their unwillingness to sacrifice only makes individual goals more difficult to achieve. One thing I believe to the fullest is that if you think and achieve as a team, the individual accolades will take care of themselves. Talent wins games, but teamwork and intelligence win championships.

29th June

There is one who scatters, yet increases more; and there is one who withholds more than is right, but it leads to poverty. The generous soul will be made rich, and he who waters will also be watered himself.

30th June

Through science, myths, and stories the reader will be guided to enter into the spirit of life and live like they have never lived before. Life will no longer be an endurance test but will become an enchantment.

We can read all the self help books and participate in powerful seminars in visioning and manifesting the vision but it would not be effective if we don't know who is visioning.

Who am I? What are my powers? How my visioning will manifest? What is this all about?

Our ability to use our computer is directly proportional to our knowledge of the operating system we are using. We must understand the operating system to produce our vision to manifestation in the shortest way efficiently.

Most of us know a piece of the operating system and what we need to do, like write a letter as we had with our typewriter before. Instead of using white out we use delete buttons. We have spell checkers etc. We feel thrilled and feel powerful. Same way after we read a good book or see a video or hear an audio.

Then there are people who know the operating system and have complete mastery over their writing, with auto-responders, editing suites and all the short cuts to produce a masterpiece.

Most of us are in first category. We know how to do certain functions mechanically and do it without knowing the operating system. We get results and feel great. We don't still have control over the computer and we use a fraction of our capabilities. We get scraps of food and not the banquet.

We try to trick our mind by continuously repeating our affirmations without knowing the operating system of the mind and get some jobs done. It is a constant struggle.

Ancient Secrets of Success for Today's World ingrains in us the operating system. It is simple, easy and imperishable. Knowing these secrets and embodying these secrets which proclaim our identity and relationship with the Universe gives us mastery over our lives.

We know who is visioning

We know what is the stuff of visioning. We know how the vision manifests so that our five senses can be engaged to relish it.

The Ancients thought out and did not compose these secrets into formulas for any marketing purpose. They were genuine and they themselves went through rigorous practice and proved it upon themselves and taught their students.

Step By Step Guidance

A whole new world awaits the reader who practices these four Ageless Secrets. They have sustained the ravages of scrutiny of the ages, since the beginning of civilization, and are Universal. They transcend all cultural and social borders. It is easy to practice and imperishable. It Works.

"Ancient Secrets of Success is for those who at times feel trapped and see no way out"

The Author guides you step-by-step in applying these principles so that you can build relationships and health, happiness and wellbeing, peace and abundance.

Tulshi Sen gives the keys to these Ancient Secrets of Success as he has received them from the Master who initiated him into the mysticism of the East and West.

Ancient Secrets of Success is for those who at times feel trapped and see no way out; whether they are surrounded by prosperity and want more from life or are in search of prosperity to complete their life.

It is for those who want to live a life of abundance, without hard work, and without the deafening tumult of anxiety that so often accompanies the search for prosperity. The Ancient Secrets bring both abundance and joy as they are both necessary for a full and a complete life.

JULY
(Life is a journey and not a destination)

<u>If life is a destination where are we heading?</u>
So many people speak of life being a journey, not a destination. I suppose if one would like to consider it a destination the final destination would be death. We are ascending towards that moment of death from the moment we are born. Death is inevitable.

The timing of our death is not something we can predict, nor is it something we can extend by eating the right things, exercising enough or avoiding any situation in life that may seem dangerous. Sudden deaths occur often and without warning to even the most cautious and healthy people.

Throughout life we've heard of children dying or being beaten to death, a young twenty year old man heavily entrenched in proper diet, exercise and without partaking in any known health risking vices, dying of brain cancer, and many more scenarios where one thought, why did this happen? Why indeed! No one can answer that question definitively!

So what about the journey in between birth and death? If we cannot possibly predict or avoid the timing of our death, why then would we become obsessed with where we are headed, the destination? Why would we put so much energy into trying to plan our futures and prevent our deaths at the expense of truly living and enjoying this glorious day before us that we have been blessed to experience?

Sadly, no one knows the answer to that question, but many can relate to those who have yet to experience and enjoy the absolute pleasures and lessons of their current journey.

Enjoying and fully experiencing the journey as it happens is not something that is easy. It is a re-learned process we must consciously undertake. Why re-learned? As children we truly do grasp the concept of the journey.

Watch a child someday. Truly watch them. They delight in every experience or encounter throughout their day from the simplicity of bubbles and balloons to the complexity of watching a spider weave his web on the other side of a window.

We cannot help but smile when we hear a child giggle from their toes as they watch bubbles magically appear from the little wand within their hand. We cannot help but comfort the child who cries unabashedly when their friend hurts their feelings. Children feel life and truly enjoy the journey, and a part of us within remembers that complete wonderment of living in the moment.

At some point in our lives, we are taught to repress these simple joys and stumbles along life's path. It is then life becomes about the destination. When we have more we will do more, when we work more we will earn more, and just in case those things do not come quickly enough, we will need to eat better, exercise more and deny ourselves simple pleasures in life so we may save for some desired pleasure down the road. What if we waste that time and tomorrow never comes?

Life is about today, enjoy it! Touch a baby, laugh with a friend, cry over a sad movie, help the poor or downtrodden, smell a flower, fly a kite, kiss your child or your parent and tell them how much you love them today, soak in a nice warm comforting bath, visit a friend who may be lonely, or a million other things that can bring us joy in this day. Most of all, love everything and everyone in life. Find joy and know peace.

We can spend the next twenty years killing ourselves with less than happiness, by denying ourselves the simple pleasure of living today, in hopes of extending our lives a few years, or we can simply choose to live our life today and fill it with all the joy and love possible. That's the journey! Enjoy it! The destination does not matter.

Yesterday is gone.

Tomorrow is not promised.

All we are truly guaranteed is right now!

Life is not a destination, Life is a journey.

1st July

For a long time it had seemed to me that life was about to begin—real life. But there was always some obstacle in the way, something to be gotten through first, some unfinished business, time still to be served, and a debt to be paid. Then life would begin. At last it dawned on me that these obstacles were my life.

2nd July

The road of life twists and turns and no two directions are ever the same. Yet our lessons come from the journey, not the destination.

3rd July

You have to let people go. Everyone who's in your life is meant to be in your journey, but not all of them are meant to stay till the end.

4th July

No one else can speak the words on your lips. Drench yourself in words unspoken. Live your life with arms wide open. Today is where your book begins. The rest is still unwritten.

5th July

It has never been, and never will be easy work! But the road that is built in hope is more pleasant to the traveler than the road built in despair, even though they both lead to the same destination.

6th July

I believe that life is a journey, often difficult and sometimes incredibly cruel, but we are well equipped for it if only we tap into our talents and gifts and allow them to blossom.

7th July

Time is a companion that goes with us on a journey. It reminds us to cherish each moment, because it will never come again. What we leave behind is not as important as how we have lived.

8th July

You are today where your thoughts have brought you; you will be tomorrow where your thoughts take you.

9th July

It takes time to build a corporate work of art. It takes time to build a life, and it takes time to develop and grow. So give yourself, your enterprise, and your family the time they deserve and the time they require.

10th July

I love the good in all the religions and respect people's religious beliefs. But, I'm more a spiritual being rather than religious. I just have one God who has no religion. My spiritual journey has faith, discipline, courage, devotion and patience. Though I don't see the entire path, I keep putting one foot in front of the other. I fall, but I rise. I'll keep rising until I finally meet my destination.

11th July

You are my ground and you are my rainbow. You are my butterfly and you are my ecstasy. You are the start of my journeys and always my destination. You are my home - the place to which I always return.

12th July

Experience is the best teacher of all. And for that, there are no guarantees that one will become an artist. Only the journey attars.

13th July

Success is not a place at which one arrives, but rather the spirit with which one undertakes and continues the journey.

14th. July

What lies behind us and what lies before us are tiny matters compared to what lies within us.

15th July

Those are a success who have lived well, laughed often, and loved much; who have gained the respect of intelligent people and the love of children, who have filled their niche and accomplished their task, who leave the world better than they found it, whether by a perfect poem or a rescued soul; who never lacked appreciation of the earth's beauty or failed to express it; who looked for the best in others and gave the best they had.

16th July

No one wants to die. Even people who want to go to heaven don't want to die to get there. And yet death is the destination we all share. No one has ever escaped it. And that is as it should be, because Death is very likely the single best invention of Life. It is Life's change agent. It clears out the old to make way for the new.

17th July

Far better it is to dare mighty things, to win glorious triumphs, even though checkered by failure, than to take rank with those poor spirits who neither enjoy much nor suffer much, because they live in the grey twilight that knows not victory nor defeat.

18th July

In any moment of decision the best thing you can do is the right thing, the next best thing is the wrong thing, and the worst thing you can do is nothing.

19th July

Lack of clarity is the number-one time-waster. Always be asking, 'What am I trying to do? How am I trying to do it?

20th July

All of life is a journey; which paths we take, what we look back on, and what we look forward to is up to us. We determine our destination, what kind of road we will take to get there, and how happy we are when we get there.

21st July

Success is not a destination, but the road that you're on. Being successful means that you're working hard and walking your walk every day. You can only live your dream by working hard towards it. That's living your dream.

22nd July

Investors have few spare tires left. Think of the image of a car on a bumpy road to an uncertain destination that has already used up its spare tire. The cash reserves of people have been eaten up by the recent market volatility.

23rd July

Too often we underestimate the power of a touch, a smile, a kind word, a listening ear, an honest compliment, or the smallest act of caring, all of which have the potential to turn a life around.

24th July

I am the largest market shareholder of clothing in the U.K. and I am not a destination shop for food. If the clothing market is affected - and it has been - and I hold my market share mathematically, then fine, I am doing no worse than the market is doing, which is exactly the case, but I'm losing revenue.

25th July

In my lifetime, I've discovered a great many incredibly talented individuals. Some have achieved stardom. Simultaneously, I've seen many dreams shattered, egos destroyed and lives changed forever. The end destination may well be fame and fortune, but the road to stardom is littered with broken hearts.

26th July

Life is part positive and part negative. Suppose you went to hear a symphony orchestra and all they played were the little, happy, high notes? Would you leave soon? Let me hear the rumble of the bass, the crash of the cymbals, and the minor keys.

27th July

I consider myself very lucky. God has a funny way of bringing some things around and knocking you in the head with the ultimate destination. Something I should have achieved quite easily took me a long time to get around to. It came in His time, not mine.

28th July

Strange is our situation here on Earth. Each of us comes for a short visit, not knowing why, yet sometimes seeming to divine a purpose. From the standpoint of daily life, however, there is one thing we do know: that man is here for the sake of other men—above all for those upon whose smiles and well-being our own happiness depends.

29ᵗʰ July

As long as we're caught up in always looking for certainty and happiness, rather than honouring the taste and smell and quality of exactly what is happening, as long as we're always running from discomfort, we're going to be caught in a cycle of unhappiness and discomfort, and we will feel weaker and weaker. This way of seeing helps us to develop inner strength. And what's especially encouraging is the view that inner strength is available to us at just the moment when we think that we've hit the bottom, when things are at their worst.

30ᵗʰ July

Whatever you do, you need courage. Whatever course you decide upon, there is always someone to tell you that you are wrong. There are always difficulties arising that tempt you to believe your critics are right. To map out a course of action and follow it to an end requires some of the same courage that a soldier needs. Peace has its victories, but it takes brave men and women to win them.

31ˢᵗ July

Life is a journey!

Of course, you have heard it all from the above quotes, it's something of a cliché. But take a moment to think about your own life. Have you "arrived" at your final destination? Have you achieved everything you've hoped to achieve? Travelled everywhere you've wanted to visit? Finished everything you've wanted to complete?

I'm willing to bet that the answer to all of these questions is "no!"

The truth is, no matter how much you achieve, accomplish, and acquire in life... there is always something more to be had. You'll never "reach" your final destination, at least not in this life!

Why does all this matter?

Because far too many people put off what really matters in pursuit of the things they want to achieve. They tell themselves that they'll worry about these things once they've reached their destination.

Things like family. Enjoying friends. Nurturing relationships. Forgiving enemies. Enjoying life. Experiencing peace.

These things are put off... and most of the time, they are never re-discovered.

However, the key to obtaining real success in our lives is to focus on enjoying the journey, taking the time to "smell the roses," and focusing on what's really important in life. This doesn't mean that we have to give up on our dreams and our goals. It's good to be ambitious; it's great to want to accomplish great things in our life. The key, however, is simply finding the right balance, discovering a mindset that allows us to pursue big things without sacrificing the "little things" that make life worth living.

Here's a little exercise for you. Take out a sheet of paper and jot down three of your biggest "life goals". These should be significant milestones... such as "buying/building my dream home" or "finding my perfect soul mate," etc. Now, on a separate section of the sheet, write down 5-10 of the most important "little things" that you don't want to forget about as you work towards these goals. Things such as: "time with my daughter/son," "nurturing relationships with friends," etc.

When you've finished this exercise, place this sheet of paper in a safe place. You will have created a visual reminder that will help you with one of life's biggest challenges; enjoying the journey in life, instead of focusing obsessively on reaching your final destination.

Sure, it's great to focus on destinations, but the most important thing is that you learn to be happy — right here and right now. I know this will be life changing for you, and also for all those in your life! Many blessings to you!

~~~~~~~~~~~~~~~~~~~~~~~~~~

This quote is something that we should all give a little thought to. <u>Life is a journey not a destination</u>. You can not go through life having desires for what you don't have. In doing so you will not see the ones you have. Enjoy your ride on this roller coaster of life. You never really know when it will come to an end.

I could never think of life as a destination, but I suppose this could be a report in how one measures success, or what they make out the meaning of their life to be. Many people struggle, lose their health, hoard, and sacrifice many values, just to arrive at what they consider happiness to be. But there is also the philosophy that says it is not where you end up in life that counts, but how you got there. Many people reach old age realizing that they wasted the best years of their life, trying to chase something that was non-existent or right in front of them the whole time.

All life is a journey, not a home; it is a road, not the country; and those transient enjoyments which you have in this life, lawful in their way—those incidental and evanescent pleasures which you may sip—are not home; they are little inns only upon the road-side of life, where you are refreshed for a moment, that you may take again the pilgrim-staff and journey on, seeking what is still before you—the rest that remained for the people of God.

The experiences are so innumerable and varied, that the journey appears to be interminable and the Destination is ever out of sight. But the wonder of it is, when at last you reach your Destination you find that you had never travelled at all! It was a journey from here to Here…

AUGUST
(When One Door Closes another Door Opens)

When one door closes another door opens, but we so often look so long and so regretfully upon the closed door, that we do not see the ones opened for us.

Most people are too attached to the past, to what they are familiar with, and therefore miss opportunities that stand right in front of them. Doors may close, but there are always other unlimited numbers of doors—new opportunities. The world is full of opportunities, if we could only see them. The Infinite Power is boundless, and so the possibilities are without number.

Not every plan works out. There are losses and failures, there are problems in relationships, loss of money or job—sometimes unpleasant things happen. We don't always have control over these happenings, but we can exercise control over our attention and attitude.

When one of these things happens, and we focus our attention on the loss—the closed door, we see only a closed door with the resultant frustration and unhappiness, but if we could only move our sight and attention away from the closed door, we might be surprised to discover a row of open new doors.

It might not be so easy to move our eyes elsewhere, due to various reasons, such as attachment to the old and familiar, and fear of the new and the unknown.

Many find it difficult to stop their stream of controlled thoughts, and consequently their mind keeps focusing on the loss, failure and frustration—the door that has closed. Will these thoughts help in anything, except creating suffering and preventing any change and improvement?

You might agree with what is being said here, but how can you free yourself from past attachments and see new opportunities? How can you bring yourself to see, and enter the new doors that open for you?

1st August

There is no key to happiness, the door is always open. On this road to happiness and fulfilment a person must be able to realize and accept a variety of things. One of these things is that a person must realize who they are, and that true happiness will only be achieved if they are willing to be themselves and not who others may want them to be!

2nd August

I long to accomplish a great and noble task, but it is my chief duty to accomplish humble tasks as though they were great and noble. The world is moved along, not only by the mighty shoves of its heroes, but also by the aggregate of the tiny pushes of each honest worker.

3rd August

Character cannot be developed in ease and quiet. Only through experience of trial and suffering can the soul be strengthened, ambition inspired, and success achieved.

4th August

Life is either a daring adventure or nothing. Security does not exist in nature, nor do the children of men as a whole experience it. Avoiding danger is no safer in the long run than exposure.

5th August

Literature is my Utopia. Here I am not disenfranchised. No barrier of the senses shuts me out from the sweet, gracious discourses of my book friends. They talk to me without embarrassment or awkwardness.

6th August

Do more than belong, participate. Do more than care, help. Do more than believe, practice. Do more than be fair, be kind. Do more than forgive, forget. Do more than dream, work.

7th August

I don't want to be labelled as one thing or another. In the past I've had successful relationships with men, and now I'm in this successful relationship with a woman. When it comes to love I am totally open. I don't want to be put into a category, as in 'I'm this' or 'I'm that'.

8th August

Life isn't meant to be easy. It's hard to take being on the top—or on the bottom. I guess I'm something of a fatalist. You have to have a sense of history, I think, to survive some of these things... Life is one crisis after another.

9th August

I'm open to whomever. I think it is absurd to assume that I have to look in a certain category. A person should make choices, about who they want to marry, who they want to spend time with, based on a variety of options, and I hope that one day people will be more open-minded about that. It's silly to look in one category or another. I would never imagine a mate based on a certain sex or race.

10th August

Talking about dreams is like talking about movies, since the cinema uses the language of dreams; years can pass in a second and you can hop from one place to another. It has a language made of image. And in the real cinema, every object and every light means something, as in a dream.

11th August

Great discoveries and improvements invariably involve the cooperation of many minds. I may be given credit for having blazed the trail, but when I look at the subsequent developments I feel the credit is due to others rather than to myself.

12th August

There is neither happiness nor misery in the world; there is only the comparison of one state to another, nothing more. He who has felt the deepest grief is best able to experience supreme happiness. We must have felt what it is to die, that we may appreciate the enjoyments of life.

13th August

You know how when you were a little kid and you believed in fairy tales, that fantasy of what your life would be, white dress, prince charming who would carry you away to a castle on a hill. You would lie in bed at night and close your eyes and you had complete and utter faith. Santa Claus, the Tooth Fairy, Prince Charming, they were so close you could taste them, but eventually you grow up, one day you open your eyes and the fairy tale disappears. Most people turn to the things and people they can trust. But the thing is it's hard to let go of that fairy tale entirely because almost everyone has that smallest bit of hope, of faith, that one day they will open their eyes and it will come true.

14th August

When you want it the most, there's no easy way out. When you're ready to go, and your heart's left in doubt. Don't give up on your faith, love comes to those who believe it...And that's the way it is.

15th August

We all live in a house on fire, no fire department to call; no way out, just the upstairs window to look out of while the fire burns the house down with us trapped, locked in it.

16th August

There are some people who live in a dream world,and there are some who face reality;and then there are thosewho turn one into the other.

17th August

Nothing happens by chance, my friend... No such thing as luck. There is a meaning behind every little thing and such a meaning behind this. Part for you, part for me, may not see it all real clear right now, but we will, before long.

18th August

An executive is a person who always decides; sometimes he decides correctly, but he always decides.

19th August

Sometimes I think you have to march right in and demand your rights, even if you don't know what your rights are, or who the person is you're talking to. Then on the way out, slam the door.

20th August

You build on failure. You use it as a stepping stone. Close the door on the past. You don't try to forget the mistakes, but you don't dwell on it. You don't let it have any of your energy, or any of your time, or any of your space.

21st August

Walk on a rainbow trail; walk on a trail of song, and all about you will be beauty. There is a way out of every dark mist, over a rainbow trail.

22nd August

If you don't go after what you want, you'll never have it. If you don't ask, the answer is always no. If you don't step forward, you're always in the same place.

23rd August

One of the great lessons I've learned in athletics is that you've got to discipline your life. No matter how good you may be, you've got to be willing to cut out of your life those things that keep you from going to the top.

24th August

When one door closes another door opens; but we so often look so long and so regretfully upon the closed door, that we do not see the ones which open for us.

25th August

All meaningful and lasting change starts first in your imagination and then works its way out. Imagination is more important than knowledge.

26th August

If it is your time love will track you down like a cruise missile. If you say 'No I don't want it right now,' that's when you'll get it for sure. Love will make a way out of no way. Love is an exploding cigar which we willingly smoke.

27th August

The sage said, "The best thing is not to hate anyone, only to love. That is the only way out of it. As soon as you have forgiven those whom you hate, you have gotten rid of them. Then you have no reason to hate them; you just forget.

28th August

Success in life has nothing to do with what you gain in life or accomplish for yourself. It's what you do for others.

29th August

It's the heart afraid of breaking that never learns to dance. It is the dream afraid of waking that never takes the chance. It is the one who won't be taken who cannot seem to give. And the soul afraid of dying that never learns to live.

30th August

Hope is the most exciting thing in life and if you honestly believe that love is out there, it will come. And even if it doesn't come straight away there is still that chance all through your life that it will.

31st August

Life can be a tough ride. It's harsh, hard and slaps you occasionally in the face. Sometimes, it seems like a never-ending struggle from one problem to another. And as if this wasn't enough already, we encounter every once in a while an incident that is so severe, so drastic and shocking that it changes our life forever. Unfortunately, in most cases this change is not for the better.

There are times in life, when a door is proverbially slammed right in front of your face. I've experienced one major life-changing event, and of course a couple of minor events that everyone else undergoes as well, like being left, given notice, stolen from, etc.

And certainly, I asked myself whenever I encountered one of these "minor life-changing events" why it was always me who had to endure such an awful thing. That was until I grew older and was confronted with a truly "major life-changing event". It did not only make me realize how insignificant most of the minor happenings were, but it also elucidated all the things I could no longer do in my life. It made me realize all the doors that had been slammed shut, never to be opened again.

I spent a lot of time in grief about all the doors that were closed and all the opportunities that were missed. It was a tough episode in my life, but time is a great healer, as they say, and so I began to make the best out my situation. And after many, many months I had learned to at least deal with the situation. But it took me a lot of reflection and courage to discover all the doors and opportunities that had presented themselves only as a result of this major life-changing event.

Only when I was brave enough to accept the situation I found myself in, only when I was courageous enough to let go of the bitterness concerning the missed opportunities, I began to discover new paths and even more exciting avenues. I do realize now that—especially this tough and difficult time—paved the way to something new and made me the person I am today. If someone would ask me if I wanted to experience a similar thing again, I would certainly answer no, as it was something you wouldn't even wish for your worst enemy. But, I wouldn't want to miss all the amazing opportunities it brought me.

There's a lesson to be learned in everything that happens to you. And it takes a lot of courage to discover the windows that were opened by such a situation. Remaining in grief and self-pity, or entirely giving up is always the easier alternative. But in reality, some doors only become opened, when an existing door is closed.

~~~~~~~~~~~~~~~~~~~~~~~~

"When one door closes another door opens." I heard it first a few years back. At the time, I was focusing so hard on the what I was losing I almost missed the meaning in the words.

However, later that day it came back to mind. For a few minutes, I wondered what they meant. I wasn't sure if the person offering them was making an observation, filling awkward silence, or making a prediction. I eventually supposed it could mean many things to different people…and moved on.

Since then, I've had the phrase revisit me several times. Each time it was for a different reason and from a different person. I have taken each opportunity to consider it from a different perspective and try to learn something. Here is what I have learned so far.

SEPTEMBER
(Wisdom to Success)

This chapter provides a summarized wisdom from literature written over the centuries on the topic that is most coveted, "What makes one successful in the shortest possible time".

In this wonderful chapter, I bring you a wealth of information that will inspire you to achieve success with wisdom in all areas: personal, professional, and spiritual. By applying these positive thoughts to your daily life, you'll find that you will not only see improvements in yourself, but you will also serve as an inspiration to those around you.

Some people have long believed in karma. They have believed that what you put out into the world will be returned to you. I certainly believe that there is quite a bit of truth to the karma bit. Even before I had known the word "karma" I tried to follow some of the best advice my wife (Mrs. Mart Koroma) gave, regarding happiness: "Do unto others as you would have them do unto you." Spread happiness and happiness will return to you. Not only does helping others make others feel good, but it is a fantastic strategy for ensuring your long-term happiness.

You will find in this chapter a collection of inspirational success quotes, sayings, and expressions. I hope to motivate and inspire you with these words of wisdom to be all that you can be. Success means different things to different people.

Whatever your thoughts on success are I hope you end up a winner, an achiever. The attainment of success is a happening in life that we should all strive for.

Being a success by achieving your goals is an occurrence that will give you confidence to continue to succeed. The antonym of failure is success. May you find prosperity and happiness in all your successes.

1st September

Sooner or later we all discover that the important moments in life are not the advertised ones, not the birthdays, the graduations, the weddings, not the great goals achieved. The real milestones are less prepossessing. They come to the door of memory unannounced, stray dogs that amble in, sniff around a bit and almost never leave. Our lives are measured by those.

2nd September

How we see failure, how we look at challenges, how we set goals—so in the end it is a combination of things not just one thing that will contribute to our success.

3rd September

The freedom to fail is vital if you're going to succeed. Most successful people fail from time to time, and it is a measure of their strength that failure merely propels them into some new attempt at success.

4th September

Prosperity is not just having things. It is the consciousness that attracts the things. Prosperity is a way of living and thinking, and not just having money or things. Poverty is a way of living and thinking, and not just a lack of money or things.

5th September

If there is any one secret of success, it lies in the ability to get the other person's point of view and see things from that person's angle as well as from your own.

6th September

Prosperity in the form of wealth works exactly the same as everything else. You will see it coming into your life when you are unattached to needing it.

7th September

There is something beautiful about all scars of whatever nature. A scar means the hurt is over, the wound is closed and healed, done with.

8th September

'Where there is a will there is a way', is an old true saying. He who resolves upon doing a thing, by that very resolution often scales the barriers to it, and secures its achievement. To think we are able, is almost to be so, to determine upon attainment is frequently attainment itself.

9th September

Feelings of worth can flourish only in an atmosphere where individual differences are appreciated, mistakes are tolerated, communication is open, and rules are flexible—the kind of atmosphere that is found in a nurturing family.

10th September

For every one of us that succeeds, it's because there's somebody there to show you the way out. The light doesn't always necessarily have to be in your family; for me it was teachers and school.

11th September

Many a man has finally succeeded only because he has failed after repeated efforts. If he had never met defeat he would never have known any great victory.

12th September

Every person who wins in any undertaking must be willing to cut all sources of retreat. Only by doing so can one be sure of maintaining that state of mind known as a burning desire to win.

13th September

Be more concerned with your character than your reputation, because your character is what you really are, while your reputation is merely what others think you are.

14th September

What this power is I cannot say; all I know is that it exists and it becomes available only when a man is in that state of mind in which he knows exactly what he wants and is fully determined not to quit until he finds it.

15th September

The man who follows the crowd will usually get no further than the crowd. The man who walks alone is likely to find himself in places no one has ever been.

16th September

The very least you can do in your life is to figure out what you hope for. And the most you can do is live inside that hope. Not admire it from a distance but live right in it, under its roof.

17th September

The crippling of individuals I consider the worst evil of capitalism. Our whole educational system suffers from this evil. An exaggerated competitive attitude is inculcated into the student, who is trained to worship acquisitive success as a preparation for his future career.

18th September

Transformation is not five minutes from now; it's a present activity. In this moment you can make a different choice, and it's these small choices and successes that build up over time to help cultivate a healthy self-image and self-esteem.

19th September

Making your mark on the world is hard. If it were easy, everybody would do it. But it's not. It takes patience, it takes commitment, and it comes with plenty of failure along the way. The real test is not whether you avoid this failure, because you won't. it's whether you let it harden or shame you into inaction, or whether you learn from it; whether you choose to persevere.

20th September

Do not save your loving speeches for you friends till they are dead; do not write them on their tombstones, speak them rather now instead.

21st September

There is no such thing as a "self-made" man. We are made up of thousands of others. Everyone who has ever done a kind deed for us, or spoken one word of encouragement to us, has entered into the make-up of our character and of our thoughts, as well as our success.

22nd September

Your work is going to fill a large part of your life, and the only way to be truly satisfied is to do what you believe is great work. And the only way to do great work is to love what you do. If you haven't found it yet, keep looking. Don't settle. As with all matters of the heart, you'll know when you find it. And, like any great relationship, it just gets better and better as the years roll on. So keep looking until you find it. Don't settle.

23rd September

How far you go in life depends on your being tender with the young, compassionate with the aged, sympathetic with the striving, and tolerant of the weak and strong, because some day in life you will have been all of these.

24th September

If a man is called to be a street sweeper, he should sweep streets even as Michelangelo painted, or Beethoven played music, or Shakespeare wrote poetry. He should sweep streets so well that all the hosts of heaven and earth will pause to say, "Here lived a great street sweeper who did his job well".

25th September

My mother drew a distinction between success and achievement. She said that success is the knowledge that you have studied and worked hard and done the best that is in you. Achievement is being praised by others, and that's nice too, but not as important or satisfying. Always aim for success and forget about achievement.

26th September

Rebellion against your handicaps gets you nowhere. Self-pity gets you nowhere. One must have the adventurous daring to accept oneself as a bundle of possibilities and undertake the most interesting game in the world—making the most of one's best.

27th September

Many of us are afraid to follow our passions, to pursue what we want most because it means taking risks and even facing failure. But to pursue your passion with all your heart and soul is success in itself. The greatest failure is to have never really tried.

28th September

Whatever your grade or position; if you know how and when to speak and when to remain silent, your chances of real success are proportionately increased.

29th September

The first rule of success, and the one that supersedes all others, is to have energy. It is important to know how to concentrate it, how to husband it, how to focus it on important things instead of frittering it away on trivia.

30th September

Everything you undergo teaches you a lesson to success. The question is: Do you have the courage to discover what lesson was taught? Are you brave enough to make use of the wisdom to success you gained?

Life can be really tough, especially in times of coping with setbacks and failures. But I know from experience: everything that happens teaches a lesson to success—whether you like the lesson or not. Often, it took me months to let go of the (ego-based) grief, self-pity and anger about what had happened. But once that work was done it gave way to a reflective approach of discovering the valuable insights and wisdoms that were taught.

Remember that this process takes a lot of time. 'Wisdom to success quotes' might not immediately catch your attention, but they will come as very profound realizations once you are ready to comprehend them. With the insight that time provides, you will be able to accept the situation and be courageous enough to let go of anger and bitterness. Only then, with an impartial point of view, profound but wise quotes to success can be drawn from the things that happened to you, hence increasing your knowledge of the important wisdom regarding life and success.

Throughout our lives we are mostly worried about things that won't happen anyway. We are afraid of failure, when in reality the regret about not having tried can be by far more painful than failure in itself. The question you have to ask yourself is whether you prefer to laugh about all the awkward failures you've experienced or to regret all the missed opportunities you rejected out of fear of failure. To me, failure is an inevitable aspect in my life. A "challenge" if you will, that I will have to face every once in a while. With it comes the realization and wisdom that the only foolproof way to avoid any kind of failure is to not try at all. The attempt to avoid failure at any cost – by not trying– is an irreversible mistake, which I regard as the worst failure of all.

OCTOBER
(Greatness and Power)

Each one of us has the power to be as great as we want to be. It is up to us to step into that greatness. No one can do it for us. We must be willing to seize the opportunities that come our way and risk going into the unknown to discover our personal greatness.

What does greatness mean to you? It may be as simple as living your life to the fullest. It may mean doing your best. Greatness doesn't mean that we have superhero powers; it means that we claim our own personal power and live life as we choose.

Greatness means something different to everyone. It is up to each one of us to discover what our greatness is and then live it. Discovering this takes time. It is a process. Once we discover what our greatness is, it will expand and we will uncover the depth of who we are.

What is your greatness?
Who are you? Do you know who you really are? How do you get to know your real self—the true self? Most of us think we know ourselves—but we do not. Many of us have limited knowledge of ourselves. We process information about our thoughts, feelings and beliefs that is in our conscious state of mind, and fail to recognize and explore information and knowledge in our unconscious mind.

Who and what we are is made up of both conscious and unconscious thoughts. The answer to the question, "Who am I?" is often hidden beyond consciousness. It is embedded in the deep valleys within your unconscious thoughts, feelings and sensations. These thoughts and feelings have become emaciated, and are not available for immediate recall to the conscious mind.

You can use the 'Quotes of Greatness and Power' below to explore the fundamental and essential characteristics of self—the nature and substance of self, and give power to your purpose and dreams, and help give birth to your greatness and Power.

1st October

It is not enough to begin; continuance is necessary. Mere enrollment will not make one a scholar; the pupil must continue in the school through the long course, until he masters every branch. Success depends upon staying power. The reason for failure in most cases is lack of perseverance.

2nd October

All great masters are chiefly distinguished by the power of adding a second, a third, and perhaps a fourth step in a continuous line. Many a man has taken the first step. With every additional step you enhance immensely the value of your first.

3rd October

Some men give up their designs when they have almost reached the goal; while others, on the contrary, obtain a victory by exerting, at the last moment, more vigorous efforts than ever before.

4th October

Life is a series of experiences, each one of which makes us bigger, even though sometimes it is hard to realize this.

5th October

Disciplining yourself to do what you know is right and important, although difficult, is the high road to pride, self-esteem and personal satisfaction.

6th October

Every single life only becomes great when the individual sets upon a goal or goals which they really believe in, which they can really commit themselves to, which they can put their whole heart and soul into.

7th October

If I had to select one quality, one personal characteristic that I regard as being most highly correlated with success, whatever the field, I would pick the trait of persistence. Determination and the will to endure to the end, to get knocked down seventy times and get up off the floor saying "Here comes number seventy-one!"

8th October

The starting point of great success and achievement has always been the same. It is for you to dream big. There is nothing more important, and nothing that works faster, than for you to cast off your own limitations and for you to begin dreaming and fantasizing about the wonderful things that you can become, have, and do.

9th October

One of the commonest mistakes and one of the costliest is thinking that success is due to some genius, some magic—something or other, which we do not possess. Success is generally due to holding on, and failure to letting go. You decide to learn a language, study music, take a course of reading, and train yourself physically. Will it be success or failure? It depends upon how much pluck and perseverance that word "decide" contains. The decision that nothing can overrule, the grip that nothing can detach will bring success. Remember the Chinese proverb, "With time and patience, the mulberry leaf becomes satin."

10th October

In art, at a certain level, there is no 'better than.' It's just about trying to operate for yourself on the most supreme level, artistically, that you can and hoping that people get it. Trusting that, just because of the way people are built and how interconnected we are, greatness will translate and symmetry will be recognised.

11th October

We have a mental block inside us that stops us from earning more than we think we are worth. If we want to earn more in reality, we have to upgrade our self-concept.

12th October

If you raise your children to feel that they can accomplish any goal or task they decide upon, you will have succeeded as a parent and you will have given your children the greatest of all blessings.

13th October

Greatness lies, not in being strong, but in the right using of strength; and strength is not used rightly when it serves only to carry a man above his fellows for his own solitary glory. He is the greatest whose strength carries up the most hearts by the attraction of his own.

14th October

With greater confidence in yourself and your abilities, you will set bigger goals, make bigger plans and commit yourself to achieving objectives that today you only dream about.

15th October

We shall not flag or fail. We shall go on to the end. We shall fight in Africa, we shall fight on the seas and the oceans, we shall fight with growing confidence and growing strength in the air, we shall defend our island, whatever the cost may be. We shall fight on the beaches, we shall fight on the landing grounds, we shall fight in the fields and in the streets, we shall fight in the hills; we shall never surrender.... And if, which I do not for a moment believe, this island or a large part of it were subjugated and starving, then our empires beyond the seas, armed and guarded by the British Fleet, will carry on the fight, until in God's own time the new world in its power and might steps forth to the rescue and liberation of the old.

16th October

You cannot control what happens to you, but you can control your attitude toward what happens to you, and in that, you will be mastering change rather than allowing it to master you.

17th October

In one of the decisive battles of World War I, disastrous reports poured into the headquarters of Marshal Foch, the commander of the Allied forces. The great general never lost heart. When things were at their worst, he drafted his famous order, which is now in all textbooks of military strategy: "My center is giving way, my right is pushed back, and my left is wavering. The situation is excellent. I shall attack!"

18th October

In life you can never be too kind or too fair; everyone you meet is carrying a heavy load. When you go through your day expressing kindness and courtesy to all you meet, you leave behind a feeling of warmth and good cheer, and you help alleviate the burdens everyone is struggling with.

19th October

From the business point of view, always encouraging the people in our company to own stock in the company, and if we're going to build something great, to have a lot of people share in the benefits of that greatness.

20th October

Try to forget yourself in the service of others. For when we think too much of ourselves and our own interests, we easily become despondent. But when we work for others, our efforts return to bless us.

21st October

People do not always understand the motives of sublime conduct, and when they are astonished they are very apt to think they ought to be alarmed. The truth is none are fit judges of greatness but those who are capable of it.

22nd October

Nothing in the world can take the place of persistence. Talent will not; nothing is more common than unsuccessful men with talent. Genius will not; unrewarded genius is almost a proverb. Education will not; the world is full of educated derelicts. Persistence and determination alone are omnipotent. The slogan, 'press on' has solved, and always will solve, the problems of the human race.

23rd October

When Babe Didrickson Zaharias, often called the Athletic phenomenon of all time, won the British women's gold tournament, people said of her what they had said many times before: "Oh, she is an automatic champion, a natural athlete." When Babe started golfing in earnest thirteen years ago she hit as many as 1,000 balls in one afternoon, playing until her hands were so sore they had to be taped.

24th October

Just as your car runs more smoothly and requires less energy to go faster and farther when the wheels are in perfect alignment, you perform better when your thoughts, feelings, emotions, goals, and values are in balance.

25th October

At most, the greatest persons are but great wens, and excrescences; men of wit and delightful conversation, but as morals for ornament, except they be so incorporated into the body of the world that they contribute something to the sustentation of the whole.

I do not think there is any other quality so essential to success of any kind as the quality of perseverance. It overcomes almost everything, even nature.

26th October

It is one of the most beautiful compensations of this life that no man can sincerely try to help another without helping himself.

27th October

Hope is important because it can make the present moment less difficult to bear. If we believe that tomorrow will be better, we can bear a hardship today.

28th October

Your choice of people to associate with, both personally and business-wise, is one of the most important choices you make. If you associate with turkeys, you will never fly with the eagles.

29th October

Your decision to be, have and do something out of ordinary entails facing difficulties that are out of the ordinary as well. Sometimes your greatest asset is simply your ability to stay with it longer than anyone else.

30th October

You have available to you, right now, a powerful supercomputer. This powerful tool has been used throughout history to take people from rags to riches, from poverty and obscurity to success and fame, from unhappiness and frustration to joy and self-fulfillment, and it can do the same for you.

31st October

Who doesn't want to be admired and honoured? Nearly everyone has a favourite star or hero they admire. It may be an athlete who has surpassed everyone else in his or her field, a performer whose talent outshines all others, an explorer who risks all to open new frontiers. We glory with them in their achievements and we mourn their passing with monuments.

This appetite for glory is more fundamental than the appetite for pleasure. Nearly everyone cherishes the secret ambition to "be somebody" and shrinks more from being "a nobody," than from suffering, pain, and material deprivation.

Make a game of finding something positive in every situation. Ninety-five percent of your emotions are determined by how you interpret events to yourself.

NOVEMBER
(From Poverty to Prosperity)

The debate about poverty and its causes rages on. On the one extreme are those who blame all poverty and its attendant ills on an oppressive "system" and tightfisted governments. These are the principled believers in socialism and the welfare state, that is, a society in which everyone is ultimately dependent on the state for security and prosperity. On the other extreme are those who are convinced that all government-operated support systems are by definition wrong and counterproductive. Individual self-reliance is held out as the only cure for poverty. The state or the individual? This is the conflict between statists and extreme individualists. It is no wonder they cannot tolerate each other.

It is not possible to debate adequately, let alone resolve, the conflict between these two extreme positions. It should be obvious that there are some people who need help because they are totally dependent and without resources of their own, including abandoned mothers and children, old people and the disabled. But it should also be obvious that the best way to escape poverty and squalor is for people to assume responsibility for themselves. This implies as a minimum that they avoid crime and drug addiction, and learn the value of honesty, loyalty and dependability.

I have listed three American success stories ("Taking Matters Into Their Own Hands") which amply demonstrate that people respond positively to opportunities for self and mutual help. A few of these are worth mentioning.

Focus Hope is a Detroit-area civil rights organization operating a machinist training program. Their goal is to help black men escape the underclass. Seven hundred trainees have been placed in well-paying auto-industry jobs. Many applicants who do not meet the minimum requirements (especially in math and reading skills) are helped to upgrade their skills. Focus Hope is also developing minority-owned businesses specializing in auto parts manufacturing. High Quality Manufacturing, staffed by former third-generation welfare mothers, recently received the Ford Motor Company's highest quality rating. It is expecting to do $4 million worth of business this year.

Parents against Drugs was organized by three women who lived in one of the worst drug-infested parts of Philadelphia. Drug dealers were terrorizing the community, even fire-bombing homes and killing children. At the women's initiative, the community began standing up to and defeating the violent drug dealers. As a result, residents gained confidence in resisting crime and soon wanted to do more to provide alternative activities, especially for the children of single welfare mothers who themselves are addicted to drugs. Neighborhood volunteers now run a youth centre and help kids with their school work, sports activities and a variety of hobbies.

Bethel New-life is a small, poor, black church in a slum section of Chicago. The members of this church decided to do something about their neighborhood, and began to raise money to purchase and renovate abandoned buildings into condominiums for low-income families. Residents, many on public assistance or making very low wages, can earn the down payment through "sweat equity" by doing some of the repair and construction work themselves. They take turns standing guard to prevent theft of equipment and materials.

All of this has given the people courage and a new pride in their own efforts and their neighborhood. So far this program has resulted in the rehabilitation of 80 co-ops and the building of 18 new houses. An additional 250 units are planned. The church has expanded its mission to include job training, health care and literacy. It even runs four businesses employing over 300 people. One spokesman for Bethel New-life said, "We're trying to show that a community-owned and controlled social-services system is more effective and less costly than the government doing it."

These stories are reassuring signs that even people in extremely adverse circumstances can overcome them if they put their minds to it and cooperate with others in the same situation. That surely must encourage all who wish for the uplifting of the poor and disadvantaged.

1stNovember

Everyday is an opportunity to have a fresh start. It doesn't matter what happened yesterday all that counts is today. When you wake up in the morning know that today is full of opportunities waiting to be grabbed. It is a new day, a new start, the beginning of a new life awaits you.

2nd November

Truth cannot be constructed. To live in ideology is, as Havel so eloquently reminds us, inevitably to live in a lie. Truth can only be revealed. We cannot be creators, only receptors. This is a situation of wealth and poverty: the one is the parent of luxury and indolence, and the other of meanness and viciousness, and both of discontent.

3rd November

Do not waste your time on Social Questions. What is the matter with the poor is Poverty; what is the matter with the rich is Uselessness. Poverty is a veil that obscures the face of greatness. An appeal is a mask covering the face of tribulation.

4th November

Ideology knows the answer before the question has been asked. Principles are something different: a set of values that have to be adapted to circumstances but not compromised away.

5th November

Dependent people need others to get what they want. Independent people can get what they want through their own efforts. Interdependent people combine their own efforts with the efforts of others to achieve their greatest success.

6th November

In public affairs men are often better pleased that the truth, though known to everybody, should be wrapped up under a decent cover than if it were exposed in open daylight to the eyes of all the world.

7th November

To be successful, you must decide exactly what you want to accomplish then resolve to pay the price to get it.

8th November

Being poor is a little like having an earache over a Bank Holiday. All you can think about is the pain and how long it will be before a healing hand can be found to take away the anguish.

9th November

I will love the light for it shows me the way, yet I will endure the darkness for it shows me the stars.

10th November

The history of the world is the history of a few people who had faith in themselves.

11th November

Of course, for a lot of people, death was a welcome change. Grinding poverty takes the edge off most things, including life.

12th November

Effective people are not problem-minded; they're opportunity-minded. They feed opportunities and starve problems.

13th November

Successful and unsuccessful people do not vary greatly in their abilities. They vary in their desires to reach their potential.

14th November

Prosperity can change man's nature; and seldom is any one cautious enough to resist the effects of good fortune.

15th November

Successful people make money. It's not that people who make money become successful, but that successful people attract money. They bring success to what they do.

16th November

If you want 1 year of prosperity, grow grain. If you want 10 years of prosperity, grow trees. If you want 100 years of prosperity, grow people.

17th November

Trust men and they will be true to you; treat them greatly and they will show themselves great.

18th November

Never be afraid to tread the path alone. Know which your path is and follow it wherever it may lead you; do not feel you have to follow in someone else's footsteps.

19th November

If the human race wishes to have a prolonged and indefinite period of material prosperity, they have only got to behave in a peaceful and helpful way toward one another.

20th November

Hard work is the price we must pay for success. I think you can accomplish anything if you're willing to pay the price.

21st November

If you have built castles in the air, your work need not be lost; that is where they should be. Now put the foundations under them.

22nd November

I am enough of an artist to draw freely upon my imagination. Imagination is more important than knowledge. Knowledge is limited. Imagination encircles the world.

23rd November

You control the ultimate result of where you will end up, what you may become and how successful you may be. No matter what our current circumstances are, always maintain a strong belief in your abilities to succeed and you will accomplish anything that you set out for.

24th November

A man is not rightly conditioned until he is a happy, healthy, and prosperous being; and happiness, health, and prosperity are the result of a harmonious adjustment of the inner with the outer of the man with his surroundings.

25th November

If virtue promises happiness, prosperity and peace, then progress in virtue is progress in each of these for to whatever point the perfection of anything brings us, progress is always an approach toward it.

26th November

The men who try to do something and fail are infinitely better than those who try to do nothing and succeed.

27th November

The main vice of capitalism is the uneven distribution of prosperity. The main vice of socialism is the even distribution of misery.

28th November

It is often better to be restricted to necessity than unconfined in the measure of our desires: prosperity destroys more individuals than adversity ruins.

29th November

Look at everything as though you were seeing it for the first time or the last time. Then your time on earth will truly be filled with glory.

30th November

There is no limit to joy when you accomplish something in life. But the initial attempt needs certain motivation which can be acquired through the 'From Poverty to Prosperity Quotes' above. People, who accomplish something in life, deserve whole hearted appreciation because it is an achievement that others have failed to do before. Accomplishment also gives a sense of satisfaction which has no substitute and is a catalyst that makes us try to achieve more and more in life.

Some of the quotes given above are the ideas of accomplished heroes and would be a great source of inspiration for those who would like to follow their footsteps. Send these quotes to your friends or anyone who wants to prove his or her hidden talents and wants accomplishments in life and to make it meaningful.

Success—'From Poverty to Prosperity' is the sweet taste that is the result of efforts taken and slightly differs from achievement. As Bo Bennett said, a dream becomes a goal when action is taken towards its success. It does not matter how many times we have failed during the process of succeeding something but the persistent endeavours only mark true success. The fact of the matter is, failures are finger posts on the road to success.

The quotes above on poverty to success are inspirational to those who want to achieve something in life and stand apart from others. It also encourages the individual to succeed more and acts as a catalyst. The recognition obtained through success is unique and brings out the best in you. But the ingredients of the magic potion of success is nothing but hard work and great effort and there are no short cuts to success.

DECEMBER
(This is the Key to Success)

Success is everybody's vision. But what is the key to success? How can you be successful? In my 'Facebook' post about defining successful people, I wrote that we should measure success based on how much we give rather than how much we receive. Fortunately, it also works nicely the other way around since those who give more almost always will also receive more. Based on that, you can see that the more value you give to others, the more successful you will be. So how do you pave your way to success? How do you become more successful? The answer is amazingly simple. Here it is:

The key to success is making yourself as useful as possible to others.
That's it. Making yourself as useful as possible to others.

If you focus on applying this, others will realize the value they get from you and they will attract more people to come to you. These new people will also realize the value they get from you and they too will attract even more people to come to you. The virtuous cycle begins and you are now on your way to success.

With this principle in mind, you should aim at increasing your usefulness to others. How do you do that? Here are some ideas:

Be observant of needs

To be useful to others, you should always be aware of even the slightest clues of needs. The more sensitive you are to the needs of others, the more appreciative people will eventually become. The best scenario is being able to anticipate a need before other people are even aware of it.

Find solutions to the needs.
Now that you are aware of needs, the next step is finding solutions to them. The solutions you offer should be as useful as possible. To be able to do so, there is no other way but to continuously build your own value. It is from the value you have that you can give value to others.

Be proactive to help
Do not wait for the other person to ask for your help. Be proactive. Give your help even before they ask.

Be sincere
What matters is not only the solution you offer, but also the way you deliver it. Being sincere means being glad to help others without expecting anything in return. Make it your joy to give something to others. People can somehow distinguish whether or not you are sincere.

Go the extra mile
Doing the above four steps is good, but add this one if you can: give more than expected. First, give what is expected, and then add a little more. If you do the above four steps people will be appreciative, but if you add this further step they will be impressed.

1st December

The difference between great people and everyone else is that great people create their lives actively, while everyone else is created by their lives, passively waiting to see where life takes them next. The difference between the two is the difference between living fully and just existing.

2nd December

Many years ago, Helen Keller was asked if she thought there was anything worse than being blind. She quickly replied that there was something much worse. She said, "The most pathetic person in the world is a person who has their sight but no vision."

3rd December

Your time is limited, so don't waste it living someone else's life. Don't be trapped by dogma - which is living with the results of other people's thinking. Don't let the noise of other's opinions drown out your own inner voice. And most important, have the courage to follow your heart and intuition. They somehow already know what you truly want to become. Everything else is secondary.

4th December

It's really important that you feel good. Because this feeling good is what goes out as a signal into the universe and starts to attract more of itself to you. So the more you can feel good, the more you will attract the things that help you feel good and that will keep bringing you up higher and higher.

5th December

You must constantly ask yourself these questions: Who am I around? What are they doing to me? What have they got me reading? What have they got me saying? Where do they have me going? What do they have me thinking? And most important, what do they have me becoming? Then ask yourself the big question: Is that okay? Your life does not get better by chance, it gets better by change.

6th December

We are not taught how to make decisions. We are not taught at school or from our parents how to earn money. We are raised that we can't have everything we want. The truth is: We can! We can have everything we are able to imagine.

7th December

Any successful person will tell you that it is easier to persuade someone to a particular course of action than to find someone who already wants to do it, but if you have not deliberately formed the habit of contacting those who need what you're offering regardless of their wants, then unconsciously you have formed the habit of limiting your contacts to those people who already want what you have to offer; and therein lies the one and only real reason for a lack of interested contacts.

8th December

I have come to believe that a great teacher is a great artist and that there are as few as there are any other great artists. It might even be the greatest of the arts since the medium is the human mind and spirit.

9th December

The critical ingredient is to stand up from where you're sitting and do something. It's as simple as that. A lot of people have ideas, but there are few who decide to do something about them now. Not tomorrow. Not next week. But today. The true entrepreneur is a doer, not a dreamer.

10th December

Set a goal to achieve something that is so big, so exhilarating that it excites you and scares you at the same time. It must be a goal that is so appealing, so much in line with your spiritual core that you can't get it out of your mind. If you do not get chills when you set a goal, you're not setting big enough goals.

11th December

The key is to just get on the bike, and the key to getting on the bike… is to stop thinking about 'there are a bunch of reasons I might fall off' and just hop on and peddle the damned thing. You can pick up a map, a tire pump, and better footwear along the way.

12th December

I made a resolve then that I was going to amount to something if I could. And no hours, nor amount of labor, nor amount of money would deter me from giving the best that there was in me. And I have done that ever since, and I win by it. I know.

13th December

Don't ever let anyone tell you that something is too competitive. Once you subtract the people who don't work very hard, or the people who aren't as good as you, your competition shrink dramatically.

14th December

Your mental picture of yourself is the key to your healthy development. You are the writer, director, and star of either an Oscar-winning epic or a Grade B movie. Who you see in your imagination will always rule your world.

15th December

The human race has had long experience and a fine tradition in surviving adversity. But we now face a task for which we have little experience, the task of surviving prosperity.

16th December

We are told that the very rich people have an extra ordinary education and that they are brilliant. But the truth is that lots of the very rich people have very little education.

17th December

Life is not easy for any of us. But what of that? We must have perseverance and above all confidence in ourselves. We must believe that we are gifted for something and that this thing must be attained.

18th December

Life is really simple as far as I'm concerned. There is no luck, you work hard and study things intently. If you do that for long and hard enough you're successful.

19th December

When you reach an obstacle, turn it into an opportunity. You have the choice. You can overcome and be a winner, or you can allow it to overcome you and be a loser. The choice is yours and yours alone. Refuse to throw in the towel. Go that extra mile that failures refuse to travel. It is far better to be exhausted from success than to be rested from failure.

20th December

I do not think there is any other quality so essential to success of any kind as the quality of perseverance. It overcomes almost everything, even nature.

21st December

It doesn't matter how many times you fail. It doesn't matter how many times you almost get it right. No one is going to know or care about your failures, and neither should you. All you have to do is learn from them and those around you because all that matters in business is that you get it right once. Then everyone can tell you how lucky you are.

22nd December

Don't let what you can't do interfere with what you can do. If you can't do something, find someone or some system that can, and you will see your business grow!

23rd December

Everybody can be great... because anybody can serve. You don't have to have a college degree to serve. You don't have to make your subject and verb agree to serve. you only need a heart full of grace. a soul generated by love.

If I had to select one quality, one personal characteristic that I regard as being most highly correlated with success, whatever the field, I would pick the trait of persistence.

24th December

Entrepreneurs are risk takers, willing to roll the dice with their money or reputation on the line in support of an idea or enterprise. They willingly assume responsibility for the success or failure of a venture and are answerable for all its facets.

25th December

One of the unique things we small companies have over the big guys is the ability to establish personal relationships. Big companies really can't do that. You read about effective organizations, learning organizations, lean and mean organizations, but small companies can be virtuous.

We as small companies can have virtue because we as small companies are basically the embodiment of one or two people, and people can have virtue, while organizations really can't.

26th December

You would not want to be rich to have money stacked somewhere. You want to be rich to be able to afford certain things (nice home, great car, beautiful clothes, expensive travels). Thinking of all this awakens an emotion in you. It is not the money, but the emotion which money represents to you.

27th December

Experience taught me a few things. One is to listen to your gut, no matter how good something sounds on paper. The second is that you're generally better off sticking with what you know. And the third is that sometimes your best investments are the ones you don't make.

28th December

You are never too old to set another goal or to dream a new dream.

We all have fear. One of the main differences between people who make great things happen in their lives, and people who never make anything happen in their lives, is being able to see past these fears so that they may soon reach their goals.

Rejection and failure will only come if you allow them to. If you are convinced that the pain of not reaching a goal in the manner that you want to is enough reason to not make any new goals or dreams, then you certainly won't make anything happen.

On the other hand, if you are convinced that no matter your age, no matter your colour, and no matter any other situation in your life, that anything is possible, your dreams new or old, will be your life.

29th December

To get what you want, you change who you are, and you change who you are by simply changing the way you think and act. And one technique for doing that which is promoted by a lot of wise teachers is to "act as if". If you "act as if" you're slim long enough, then one day you will attract slimness even though you may be 100 pounds overweight today. If you act as if you're wealthy long enough, then one day you will attract all the wealth you can imagine even though you may this moment be destitute and homeless.

30th December

You don't need a ton of resources to see your dream come to fruition. You just need a vision and the willingness to work hard. Remember that some of the most successful companies started in basements, so don't discount your idea just because you don't know how to implement it yet.

31st December

Bluntly, vision is the eyesight or the key to success. But it also refers to the farsightedness or the forethought. We have to envision the future to make our dreams come true. Vision helps us to draw a clear picture of our goals and ambitions. Then we can chalk out the actions to be taken to achieve the ambition.

Joel barker clearly states "vision without action is a dream. Action without vision is simply passing the time. Action with vision is making a positive difference". There is no limit to our vision and the extent of our vision decides the extent of our key to success. We are limited not by our abilities but by our vision. Vision is not possessed by all. Only those who are determined to set a goal in life and work hard towards it, have a vision, for it is the key to success.

Don't confuse your path with your destination; just because it's stormy now doesn't mean you aren't headed for sunshine. Just because you are in a period with a lot of storms, or a lot of trials, doesn't mean that a sunny time isn't ahead. It just means that you are going through some things, and that changing your outlook may help you a lot in overcoming a destructive mindset.

A destructive mindset is a mindset that doesn't allow you to see the light ahead, and fools you into thinking that you are worse off than you really are in most cases.

Never confuse where you are now, with where it is you want to be. This is a new day, and only you can live the way you need to achieve and soar to new heights. Be that unrelenting spirit that you know you can really be as each day passes. Work hard daily, and continue to stay focused on obtaining the life that you want for you and the people who matter most to you.

RECAPPING

The Gradual Nature of Success

When we think about success and look at the achievements of successful people, all we can see is the superficial layer. We see the successful business, the bestselling novel, or the artistic masterpiece. Naturally, we assume that success requires a similar achievement and we're discouraged because, as beginners, we're incapable of reaching such heights.

This is when most people start thinking in terms of "can't". If we could see successful people as beginners and understand every tiny effort that gradually contributed to their success, we wouldn't be discouraged by our own initial ignorance. Instead of seeing the path to success as a gargantuan wall, we'd see it as a very long but climbable staircase.

Unlike a system with rules and procedures, the optimization mentality is a philosophy that can be applied to anything. The toughest part is thinking independently and motivating yourself to take action. These four ways of thinking all contribute to the optimization mentality.

1. Keep an open mind — It's impossible to improve when you aren't looking for opportunities. Don't stunt your own growth by believing you've already reached the top of the ladder. There is always some small way to get better. Keep your eyes and ears open so you don't miss it, and seriously consider even the strangest sounding ideas.

2. Stimulate your mind — We get better as we get smarter. Be curious. Experiment with different options until you find the best. Watch what other people are

doing, preferably smart people. Read books and articles on a wide variety of topics. Follow up on the ideas that pop into your head at 3 a.m.

3. Seek advice from superiors — For every aspect of your life, chances are you know at least one person who is a little bit better in that area. Ask your friend in finance how to invest. Ask your engineer brother-in-law what computer to buy. Leveraging the knowledge of others is the fastest way to improve.

4. Never be satisfied — Don't settle for mediocrity. We should be grateful for our good fortune, but we shouldn't stop trying to get better. Once we become satisfied we start stagnating. The world is constantly moving. If you aren't moving with it you're falling behind.

I already know what the trolls are going to say, "Everything in this book is completely obvious." No kidding. There is a big difference between understanding a concept on an intellectual level and taking it to heart. The optimization mentality is easy to grasp, but comprehending it's importance and implementing it on a day to day basis isn't. If it was there wouldn't be so many people wondering what went wrong.

Embracing the optimization mentality is something everyone should strive for. Every productive action is driven by the goal of continuous improvement. That's why 'Oracle of Success' is dedicated for you to succeed in your goals.

Alphabet of success

Don't waste your time worrying about what might have been, and if you slip just get back on the road again. Though the winter sky claims the summer's blue, to yourself you must still be true. For you have dreams of success that will never pass away and they will remain your lasting sun through poverty's way.

A – Art

Art of success...It is amazing what you can accomplish when you do not care who gets the credit.... I don't think of all the misery but of the beauty that still remains.

B – Believe

Believe In You... Some people won't believe in you; they won't encourage you to succeed, but you must always believe in you, no matter how long the journey ahead seems. Some people will be jealous of you; their words will be sharp and unkind, but you must close your ears to such words, and never allow them to change your direction or your mind.

C – Change

Change things…There are many things that catch your eye, but only a few that will catch your heart. Pursue them. Change your thoughts and you change your world. If you don't like something, change it. If you can't change it, change the way you think about it.

D – Discipline

Discipline... If you're not willing to accept your own discipline, you're not going to accomplish two percent of what you could—and you're going to miss out on 98% of the good things you could have.

E – Expect

Expect...Expect a rainbow, and you'll find it eventually.... There's no easy way out. If there were, I would have bought it. And believe me, it would be one of my favorite things!

F – Fortunate

Fortunate People...Fortunate is the person who has developed the self-control to steer a straight course towards his objective in life, without being swayed from his purpose by either commendation or condemnation.

G – Great

Greatest Discovery...Great things are not done by impulse, but by a series of small things brought together.... The greatest discovery of my generation is that a human being can alter his life by altering his attitudes.

H – Hope

Hope and Success...You're feeling lonely, a victim of the blues... Your burden is so great that you don't know what to do. But you can lighten your load and escape your despair, by asking for God's assistance in a heartfelt prayer.

I – Increase

Increase your speed...Begin doing what you want to do now. We have only this moment, sparkling like a star in our hand, and melting like a snowflake. There is more to life than increasing its speed.

J – Jump

Jump and be Happy...Put your heart, mind, intellect, and soul even to your smallest acts. This is the secret of success. If you refuse to accept anything but the best, you'll get the best. Begin to live as you wish to live. Success is doing ordinary things extraordinarily well.

K – Keep

Keeping Hope... Hope is a state of mind, not of the world. Hope, in this deep and powerful sense, is not the same as joy that things are going well, or willingness to invest in enterprises that are obviously heading for success, but rather an ability to work for something because it is good.

L – Laziness

Lazy Life...Laziness is nothing more than the habit of resting before you get tired. What you make of your life is up to you. You have all the tools and resources you need. Your answers lie inside of you. It's not hard to make decisions when you know what your values are.

M – Many

Many Dreams...The clock is always ticking, and the sand runs out too fast. You should begin today before today becomes the past... Just take your dream and keep on moving. There's no time to stop and stare.... Look at the cemetery—many dreams die there.

N – Never

Never Believe It...The reason most people never reach their goals is that they don't define them, or ever seriously consider them as believable or achievable. Winners can tell you where they are going, what they plan to do along the way, and who will be sharing the adventure with them.

O – Obstacle

One Step of Obstacle...Obstacles cannot crush me. Every obstacle yields to stern resolve. Defeat may test you; it need not stop you. If at first you don't succeed, try another way. For every obstacle there is a solution. Nothing in the world can take the place of persistence. The greatest mistake is giving up.

P – Progress

Progress...No problem was ever solved without a climb, and every mountain can only be tackled one step at a time. Though burdens bring disappointment and pain, a summit lies ahead to gain.

Q–Quality

Quality of Success... Bad things do happen; how I respond to them defines my character and the quality of my life. I can choose to sit in perpetual sadness, immobilized by the gravity of my loss, or I can choose to rise from the pain and treasure the most precious gift I have—life itself.

R – Reflect

Reflection Success...What this power is I cannot say; all I know is that it exists and it becomes available only when a man is in that state of mind in which he knows exactly what he wants and is fully determined not to quit until he finds it.

S – Self-control

Secret of Self-control...I define self-control, in the beginning of life, as the choice of succeeding what I really want by doing things I really don't want to do. Once this becomes a habit, discipline becomes the choice of succeeding what I really want by doing the very things I now want to do! I really believe that a disciplined life becomes a joy—but only after we have worked hard to practice it. Every day may not be good, but there's something good in every day.

T – Time

Time and Tide...In truth, people can generally make time for what they choose to do; it is not really the time but the will that is lacking. When you get in a tight place and everything goes against you, till it seems as though you could not hold on a minute longer, never give up then, for that is just the place and time that the tide will turn.

U–Unlimited

Unlimited… You are everything that is, your thoughts, your life, your dreams come true. You are everything you choose to be. You are as unlimited as the endless universe.

V– Victory

Victory… The victory of success is half won when one gains the habit of setting goals and achieving them. Even the most tedious chore will become endurable as you parade through each day, convinced that every task, no matter how menial or boring, brings you closer to achieving your dreams.

W – Women

Women… Women face enough pressures and challenges in a workplace that is still depressingly biased against a female's success. Add to that, the fact that the very thing many women I know find most rewarding (having kids) is now frowned upon.

X – X-ray

X-ray your life… Too many people spend money they haven't earned, to buy thing they don't want, to impress people they don't like.

Y – You

You will find… as you look back upon your life, that the moments when you really lived are the moments when you have done things in the spirit of love.

Z – Zeal

The generous wish to share with all what is precious, to spread broadcast priceless truths, to shut out none from the illumination of true knowledge, has resulted in a zeal without discretion that has vulgarised Christianity, and has presented its teachings in a form that often repels the heart and alienates the intellect.

Never Too Old To Succeed

You may be right now heading for your fifties and you are wondering to yourself if you will ever succeed in realising your long held dreams.

There is something you have always wanted to do. It could be a business idea you believe would bring a solution to a problem of millions of people; it could be to travel the world and see other places and culture; or to get to the pinnacle of your career. It could even be a noble course to serve humanity—to reach out to people who are in need and bring help to them.

Whenever you visualise yourself doing this thing, you are filled with joy and fulfilment. No doubt, if you can live this life of your dreams, you will have considered your life here on earth successful. But the problem is that you just have not been able to even start doing it.

Now, you look in the mirror and you see the tell-tale signs of aging on your face, and you are gripped with fear that you might not be able to make that dream happen after all. Your spirit is low whenever you realise how old you are becoming, and your enthusiasm for the object of your dream is dampened.

But wait a minute; I have something to tell you, you're never 'too old to succeed' in life! I have to restate it to emphasise the fact that whatever age you are now, as long as you are alive, you can still achieve success and live the life of your dreams. There have been people who came to phenomenal success, not when they were young, but surprisingly when they were in their "old age", an age when they would have been expected to start preparing to jet out of the earth.

Here are some examples that you're 'Never too old to succeed':

At age 40, Hank Aaron hit his 715th home run, more than anyone had ever hit.

At age 41, Christopher Columbus landed in the New World.

At age 44, Marie Curie won the Nobel Prize in chemistry.

At age 49, Mario Puzo published 'The Godfather'.

At age 52, Ludwig Van Beethoven composed the Ninth Symphony.

At age 53, Margaret Thatcher was elected Prime Minister of Britain, the first woman to hold that office.

At age 55, Alex Haley published 'Roots'.

At age 57, Annie Peck climbed Mount Huascaran in the Andes. She was the first person to reach the top.

At age 59, Clara Barton founded the Red Cross.

At age 63, Francis Galton revealed to the world that no two people have the same fingerprints and revolutionized crime fighting in the process.

At age 64, John Pierpont Morgan formed U.S. Steel, the world's first billion dollar corporation.

At age 65, Laura Ingalls published 'Little House In the Big Woods', the first story in the popular 'Little House on the Prairie,' series.

At age 68, Clifford Batt swam the English Channel.

At age 69, Mother Teresa won the Nobel Peace Prize.

At age 74, Nelson Mandela became the oldest elected president of South Africa in 1994.

At age 78, Grandma Moses began taking painting seriously. Soon afterward, her career took off.

At age 79, Benjamin Franklin invented the bifocals.

At age 94, Leopold Stokowski signed a six-year contract to conduct music.

At age 100, Ichijirou Araya climbed Mount Fuji.

www.ingramcontent.com/pod-product-compliance
Lightning Source LLC
Chambersburg PA
CBHW022108090426
42743CB00008B/763